PATIENT ACTIVATION

The 4 Steps Proven to Move Health Care Consumers From Awareness to Activation

**BOB BAURYS
& MARK STINSON**

83bar, LLC | Austin, Texas

Praise for 83bar and Its Patient Activation Process

Performance:

You guys do a fantastic job at 83bar...we did not expect such a good turn around.

J. P., Research Coordinator

One of our candidates mentioned her patient journey with 83bar and how easy it was to be directed to a specialist on her radio show!

Charita, Research Coordinator

83bar never disappoints; you're always 10 steps ahead – whether it's site management, handling the RCs and Clinical team, campaign optimization, performance analysis and weekly reports, global expansion or budget planning. I know I can always trust and rely on 83bar as my strategic partners.

Amy, Global Market Dev. Consultant

Account Management:

Thank you so much for all of your help and complete thoroughness through this process!

Wendy, Market Development Manager

Everything is running smoothly. Thank you so much for being available to help, even when you're on vacation. We really appreciate it!

Jake, Clinical Specialist

Creative:

The ads featuring Dr. C.T. are Rock Star! I did not expect to see the ad. I shared it with the whole office!

Marsha, Practice Manager

Positive Feedback from Patient Prospects

Thank you for caring so much about a stranger. You don't find people like you. You're more of a legend that still lives.

Kyphoplasty

You called me at the perfect time, when I was struggling with lifestyle changes and decision making. Thank you for giving me continuing support and information! Grateful to you for your role in the procedure. I will report in with the step by step outcome!! Thanks so much!

Bladder Control

The patient lead had hiatal hernia repair and TIF procedure with Dr. P. Stated that Dr. P. is a wonderful doctor.

GERD

The patient lead was tested at the time of her appointment. She said Dr. S. was fabulous and explained everything really well to her.

Genetics

The patient lead is very happy with the office and would give Dr. G. a 10 on a 1-5 scale. Had TIF procedure done and is doing very well.

GERD

Dedication

To my wife, Claudette, who has put up with untold hours, financial risks, and exhaustion to get to this point.

To my business partners who have shored up my weaknesses and allowed this journey to happen.

To the 20,000-plus patients whom we have served directly. You taught me the value of plain, straightforward information and viewing life through their eyes.

Contents

Foreword

Nothing is more important and personal in our lives than our health and the health of those whom we love. At this moment in time, it is exciting to learn and consider all of the ways to improve health.

From biological medicines to genome sequencing to robotic surgery, the pace of innovation to help us better manage our quality of life is accelerating faster than ever before. Terms like "personalized medicine" and "precision cancer therapy" which were once seen only in peer-reviewed journals and scientific posters have become part of the vocabulary for average citizens and mainstream media organizations.

I have had the privilege of working with many innovators in biotech, large pharma, medical devices, artificial intelligence, and many more sectors. Capital has poured into these areas and many of our most intelligent and motivated leaders have taken up the challenge of moving these technologies from ideation to impact. But there has always been something missing.

Throughout history, we humans have tended to be attracted to the shiny object. That is natural as we are an inherently curious species, continually trying to push our own evolution. However, in this quest to truly change the world or discover the next great technological advancement, we often cannot see the forest for the trees.

I recently had the honor and privilege to work for and alongside two of the world's greatest scientific minds, Dr. J. Craig Venter and Dr. Hamilton Smith. Dr. Venter has talked often of personalizing care and at the center of this has always been the human genome—ever since he was the first to sequence it back in 2001. While our genetics are important, they only tell part of the story. Catching disease early, diet, environment, our metabolism, our microbiome, and many more factors play equal if not greater roles in our overall health and longevity. There is not a single pill for health. For that reason, I forced myself to take a step back and ask, "How do we really start to personalize care—from a small tweak to a diet to a complicated brain surgery? How do we help patients recognize potential health issues sooner, get them to the right specialist quickly, ensure the right intervention is offered, and stay with that patient as they navigate the health care system?"

All the innovation we see today amounts to a very large, very exciting tool box, a tool box that no single physician or even hospital system has the expertise to fully utilize, assuming they even have knowledge that the tools exist to begin with. So, the question becomes: If innovation is so rapid that our physicians and trained professionals do not fully understand what is available for their patients, how do we ensure that each person is receiving the best care available?

To answer that question, we must first define the goal. That goal is to treat a patient as a customer, getting them from where they are today to well as quickly and efficiently as possible. Success and speed in this journey must also align the incentives for all stakeholders: empowering patients to take control of their health, preparing patients and providers with the information they need to ensure efficient consultations and actions, bridging the information gap between innovators and those they hope to heal, and ultimately lowering the overall cost of health for the consumer.

This seems like a tall order until you get away from the thinking that has plagued health care systems to date: the concept of "population" health care with its focus on incidence rates and treating the masses in a similar fashion. It is perfectly logical why innovators and providers went down this path—the belief was that this approach would lead to the most improved outcomes for the largest number of people. Made sense to me as well, until I realized that many patients are square pegs who do not fit into those round holes. They bounce around the system, often taking months if not years to arrive at an intervention that works for them. After nearly a decade on Wall Street advising some of the largest and most innovative companies in health care, I saw countless failed attempts to right all these wrongs. I actually concluded that companies taking a population approach and improving that system over time was likely our best bet.

Then I met a company in Austin, Texas, that flipped this entire thinking on its head: 83bar.

What if we could treat each patient as what they are—a unique n of 1—and do so by leveraging technologies employed by other industries to personalize experiences?

Health care companies do a fairly good job of making patients aware that there are innovations out there. However, TV commercials, internet ads, conference presentations, and marketing campaigns cannot hope to be directed at the individual. In addition, these approaches rarely bring a patient into the system to better their health. We need an approach that takes these individuals from being aware to a state of activation, ready to take control of their health for the better.

The concept of patient activation is a widely recognized concept but helping to bring patients the confidence to take a more active role in managing their health has always been a limitation—until today.

The team at 83bar has developed a fully-enclosed, technology-enabled, HIPAA-compliant system to provide empathetic clinical education and concierge services to patients at scale. By partnering with innovators and providers, not to sell their products or services, but rather to educate and empower the masses, the team has seen amazing results—and more important, amazing patient outcomes. Activating patients to become consumers of health care, improving provider workflows, and finding the right intervention for each patient is now possible.

While whole genome sequencing is sexy and can tell you a lot about your health and your risks, genetics is not personalized medicine. Personalized medicine is leveraging all the tools at our disposal to get each individual patient from where they are today to the wellness they want, as efficiently as possible.

83bar's patient activation approach is truly personalized care.

Ben Chiarelli
Founder and Chief Executive Officer, Cellibre

Introduction

A perfect storm of factors rocks the health care world.

In the medical market today, companies and consumers are engaged in a skirmish upon a schism of ever-shifting sand.

For the consumer, enormous quantities of uncurated information are more distracting than helpful. You struggle to separate the truth from the untruth while wading through unfamiliar terms and a cost structure that is intimidating even to those on the upper rungs of the economic ladder.

You realize that the system is biased toward leading you to make decisions that blend what's best for you with what's best for your health care provider. Sometimes the benefits scale is equally balanced—sometimes it is not. Those who have unbiased information are more likely to win.

It should be a ripe market for purveyors of health care services and products—unending need, mass confusion, rapid advancements, and an ever-changing landscape. Providers and suppliers should be holding most of the cards.

However, market currents move too swiftly for all parties involved. Both sides of the equation are therefore struggling to find their footing in the new paradigm.

If you're a provider or a manufacturer and you're trying to attract consumers, you are struggling with six key issues:

- **Consumer tolerance is changing.** You have to create the demand and understand how people self-manage themselves. With $5,000 and $10,000 deductibles, health care has become a consumer retail decision. What used to be an automatic decision because "My doctor told me I needed this" is now a seriesb of mini discussions and cost-benefit analysis with multiple participants, often including family, providers, insurers, and even employers.

  Now getting a procedure or surgery that is the least bit elective is much more like an Amazon-type of thought process environment (research, reviews, feedback comparisons); it is no longer the old, "I don't care, I'm going to get it done because my insurance is going to pay for it." The times have changed as has the environment.

- **Attention spans are shortening.** You need to understand the level and capability of your prospective consumers' knowledge retention. What does the prospective patient know as a baseline? What are they willing to learn? What can they retain? Are they only willing to scan information and in what format? Old style content delivery is dead. I preach "One sentence, three bullets, one sentence" to my team often. We have found that to be the effective threshold of the US consumer, given the avalanche of information they receive every day.

- **There is a shortage of those who have even a modicum of understanding of the healthcare market.** Therefore it is more important than ever to know who the real decision-maker is whom you should be conversing with. Hint: In most households, the 45 to 60-year-old female often makes decisions for herself, her spouse, her family, her parents, and her in-laws. Yes, even for men's health issues.

- **Understand the resistance your prospective consumers will encounter along the way**, from initial engagement to scheduling, and even dealing with the front desk of many providers.

- While accepting the given fact that there is little time for patient education in the treatment process, you still need to understand how your consumers learn and what they are willing to do to make an impact on their health. **You need to invest in patient education**, for prepared patients create far less friction in an organised treatment flow.

You are working with little data in an industry that should be driven by data. The industry data-wise is much further behind other industries than one would expect given the large number of expenditures. The concept of "art of medicine" has been pervasive for a long time.

What it is like to be a patient today

Basically there are two types of patients in the health care system. Though not perfect, trendwise these descriptors are accurate.

Traditional Pathway Patient — a consumer who begins their journey immediately by talking to their doctor about a medical issue; timewise, from initial thought process or incident to actual resolution, this pathway can take years (definitely months, but often years) between when someone goes into the doctor's office, they're managed, they're referred, they get on the first round of meds, and when they're finally referred to a specialist. Finally, the treatment options are shared and the patient has the procedure or medication is modified. There are several gaps in this journey where the consumer is left unmanaged and to their own devices.

Self-Managed Pathway Patient — a patient self-manages their own health care pathway; it's a very similar, long, and involved process, the key exception being that they are seeking counsel from their trusted circle. They look for answers before they walk into a physician's office with stacks of paper and start asking questions. They seek opinions, do their own research then they finally make a decision. Again, this takes a lot of time and there's no quality control over the information they're reviewing, nor do they have the native ability to prioritize their findings.

In this context we at 83bar created our system and we work diligently every day to address these factors as part of our process.

Why I write about Patient Activation

My personal story includes getting sick fifteen years ago and dealing with the stress and frustration of not knowing what was wrong with me. Going from working eighty hours a week to not being able to get off the couch, I began to see I was entering into a medical model that didn't have time to figure out my complicated condition. So, my blood tests all came back normal, all of my diagnostic tests came back normal, and I still didn't feel well. I've been a person who has been highly functional their whole life, but I was running out of ideas and out of pathways.

The scariest part is that after spending nearly twenty years in the health care business, I had many close relationships within the community. Yet I was still not getting any answers—even when calling in the "friend card."

I started to realize that the only way I had a chance of getting better was to find someone who would actually spend the time and effort to individually work with me.

You might relate to this. The more I talked with others, the more I knew I wasn't alone in my experiences.

At this point, I began looking for doctors who were more integrative and holistic, and I started to look for physicians who would look deeper. I found an array of skills, knowledge, and cost structures that was even surprising for me—a twenty-year grizzled veteran of the health care marketplace.

When I went to "regular" physicians, it felt like the visit cost virtually nothing or was near free because insurance would pay. But when I started going to people who were focused on the symptomatology that I was struggling with, I was paying $3,000 and $4,000 per visit for forty-minute visits, and they were literally the only options. I remember sitting in one of the offices of one of these specialists in West Virginia; Rod Stewart's second wife was the only other person sitting in the office with me. This was fifteen years ago. When she introduced herself, I realized that access to specialists in integrative medicine was what I called "rockstar medicine" for the extremely wealthy. Or for people like me, who were so desperate they were willing to bet it all to try to get better. First I was stunned and then I got mad.

I didn't perceive the regular mass product to be good at fixing ailments that were out of the norm, but "rockstar medicine" should have been accessible to more people. I was so mad, I called my business partner on the way from an appointment and told her our next company had just "found us." And that was the start of Fibromyalgia and Fatigue Centers.

We began to build Fibromyalgia and Fatigue Centers (FFC) with the idea that we could form a model that wouldn't be $3,000 an hour, but rather $350 an hour—one-tenth the cost. Make it available to the masses, but make the appointments 45-60 minutes and try to bring the best of all worlds:

- Give physicians the ability to practice the art of medicine, focusing on patients and their needs rather than catering to the reimbursement schedules of insurers.

- Provide a platform for patients who had complicated conditions that needed attention and, often times, research.

- Create an environment that was healthy for practitioners as well as patients.

Along the way, we found a mechanism to locate and educate patients who were willing to carve out some of their disposable income because their health was that important to them and they understood the value of focused time and attention in the US health care system.

Then we were fortunate to find a group of forward-thinking physicians who were willing to break the paradigm of forty or fifty patients a day to treat six or eight patients a day. These physicians choose to actively do more critical thinking and continue their education in a quest to be as knowledgeable as possible in order to deliver leading-edge medical care.

That is the genesis of the Patient Activation process.

I've spent the last fifteen years working on my own health as well as building medical businesses around many diseases and conditions. My idea was that if I can build a medical model that addresses difficult condition and disease types, focusing on meeting the needs of both the patient and the physician, it would be very meaningful and life-valuing work. Once developed—if that model could be replicated—that is an even better paradigm: helping even more people.

Yes, it might be more expensive than mass-produced medicine. But at the same time, the outcomes will usually be better, even ten to fifteen times more substantial. Most of all, the patient experience will be significantly better, as will physician satisfaction levels.

A Libertarian at heart, it is important to me that people have a choice with regard to the decisions revolving around taking care of their health. Consumers themselves should decide what is right for them— not some insurance company and not some authoritative physician personality. I truly believe consumers have the right to make unbiased, educated health care decisions based on what is most important in their lives.

Market forces—including self-directed consumers, rising friction pricing rates, and availability of knowledge once only held by professionals—are setting the stage for massive change in the next decade. It won't be easy and it won't be linear but it will be worth it.

How I see the way forward

I feel patient activation is the future, patient activation in the sense of enabling a prospective patient to go from the state of awareness (I know of, I've heard about, etc.) to the actual state of engagement with a solution.

In the past, when low deductibles and minimal co-pays were the norm, American health care was a model derived from a "funny money" insurance system. While most consumer decisions are made via a cost-benefit analysis, the proverbial thumb was on the scale when the cost to the patient was insignificant.

This patient dynamic is changing, yet so many providers and staff working in the current system haven't been trained with the skills for making the conversion to a consumer-oriented process.

Given that, we're already experiencing an incredible amount of pain in this space which will continue for the next ten to fifteen years. There is no question in my mind the transition will be made, and there is a significant amount of opportunity for people who learn how to make that transition quickly and adapt to it. On the other hand, there's a significant amount of pain, as there already has been, for people who are not capable of making or not willing to make that transition. They may still be longing for the way it was.

Patient Activation is the way forward. It cannot—nor will it—be stopped.

PART I:

THE ESSENTIALS OF PATIENT ACTIVATION

Chapter 1:

PATIENT ACTIVATION from the Health Care Consumer's Point of View

Only recently has the medical community begun to see patients as health care consumers rather than mere subjects of office visits or procedures. The concept of patient activation begins with an emphasis on consumer-driven care and the principles of a consumer-centered experience.

When viewed this way, the providers of care (plus the makers of therapies and devices) can deliver more responsive and personalized care that helps patients recognize and develop their own strengths and abilities. This is the underpinning of an approach to support people in the development of the ability to better manage their own health by giving them information they can understand and act upon.

Concept: Implement and replicate a framework

In this book, you'll learn the definitions behind the four-point process of PATIENT ACTIVATION. I will also share how 83bar clients (as well as other leading health care organizations) successfully use the model in a wide range of initiatives. To effectively illustrate many of the points, we will follow the journey of Susan, a prototypical patient who moves from suffering pain, fear, and embarrassment to enjoying confidence and relief as she is equipped with knowledge and support. Her story represents the experience of patients who have been empowered by PATIENT ACTIVATION. Along the way, you will learn specific techniques for applying the PATIENT ACTIVATION yourself.

The concept of patient activation has gained credence among clinicians, academics and think-tanks worldwide. So, it is a widely accepted phrase that is certainly not owned by any one company. However, at 83bar, we recognized that the term may be conceptual without a framework for implementation and replication. that is why the idea of activating patients needed to move beyond simply helping people overcome inaction or lack of resources.

In this book, PATIENT ACTIVATION will refer to a fully integrated system to move from awareness to action. It includes a step-wise process supported by a set of customized software and proprietary tools. This system and four-point model was designed to standardize and automate most of the key functions involved. Of course, I'm very proud of what has been created and enhanced over many years of development. But it's not my intention to simply sell our offering. Rather, it is to reveal the principles and philosophies that are the foundation of our approach. In this way, you can learn the approach and find ways to implement it in your own situation.

PATIENT ACTIVATION Process Overview

What It Is	A fully integrated 4-part system designed to transition people from being passive patients to active consumers of health care.
What It Does	Creates a structured set of tools and communication methods to enhance the knowledge, skills, and confidence of a person in managing their health.
How to Use It	To attract and connect patients in need of condition-specific treatments, diagnostics, or devices with a clinic or practitioner providing health care solutions.
Why It Is Different	Provides and manages the full spectrum of online prospect identification, health assessment, nurse-staffed call center for clinical consultations, business intelligence, and analytics.
Why that Difference is Meaningful to the Consumer	While patient activation is closely linked to other concepts such as 'self-efficacy' and 'readiness to change,' it is a broader and more general concept, reflecting attitudes and approaches to self-management and engagement with health and health care, rather than being tied to specific behaviors. It's empowering to be educated and prepared to act.

Why that Difference is Relevant to Providers and Brands	Traditionally, patient education was done through physician engagement and support materials. That method is completely broken. It is no longer enough to create consumer awareness of your brand/service/device etc. Today, it takes more to win in this hyper-competitive environment.

The Patient Activation System in Four Parts

Let's start with an overview of the PATIENT ACTIVATION process. The process encompasses four parts: Locate, Educate, Navigate, and Advocate. (Later chapters will cover each step in greater detail.)

1. Locate

Purpose: To identify and engage prospective patients before they enter into the traditional health care ecosystem so that we might be able to shorten their journey to health through education, curated information and navigation.

Action: We identify prospective patients through risk assessment and health surveys.

Then, we respond to them very quickly (usually within minutes) with registered nurses who have a high degree of experience.

2. Educate

Purpose: To provide a highly personalized education process that utilizes prospective patient input from risk assessments/health surveys, curated information, and an empathetic delivery from a health care professional.

Action: We share relevant information with patients, offer meaningful solutions, and help them make informed decisions.

3. Navigate

Purpose: To provide navigational assistance and options once the basis for an informed decision has been made.

Action: We guide patients to action through appointment scheduling or service fulfillment, whichever is appropriate for the client.

4. Advocate

Purpose: To provide a feedback loop to allow the patient to either amplify their positive feelings about the relationship or take corrective actions should something be amiss.

Action: We offer comprehensive follow-up to ensure patient satisfaction with their experience and to promote improved treatment and health care.

When this complete process is applied, it makes an impact on everyone in the health care continuum:

- It's activating—for the health care consumer.

- It's also activating—in the world of the provider and staff.

- It's meaningfully activating—when the two interact.

And I don't just say that with the passion of a marketer and operator. The conclusions and results shared in this book are documented from an array of sources, including a literature review of major academic journals, trade publications, branding books, and specific case studies from our experience with dozens and dozens of programs. We've had a chance to do market research and analytics that have taught us a lot of lessons. Plus, our company has had the privilege of having worked with more than 50 clients and brands.

A potential activated health care consumer

At the heart of it all, I believe the consumer is a person first. When that person becomes a health "seeker," they start a search that we can help with because we understand the journey.

Since we've worked across twenty different health care categories, we empathetically understand who this person is and what they feel. We can tell from the statistics we've gathered how best to describe them in terms of:

Demographics

- Age

- Income

- Occupation

- Location

- Education

- etc.

Psychographics

- Lifestyles

- Hobbies

- Family

- Activities

- etc.

The average health care "target" for activation is usually a 45 to 60-year-old woman. Beyond just taking care of herself, she is managing the health of children in her household up to twenty-five years old. She's also managing her spouse's or partner's health care. She's managing the health care of her parents and usually her partner's parents. Taken together, she is the key decision-maker in the entire extended family.

This woman is taking a reasonably rational approach, willing to do the research but keenly aware that she doesn't know everything. She is usually someone who wants to have education, yet not be told what to do. She tends to be a critical thinker in the family and wants to understand what the options are. She filters what she has been told, and then makes the decision. She will help guide other family members through the process. that is our profile of the typical target of patient activation efforts.

As odd as it seems, even if you're selling prostate-related services, you would think that you're speaking to mostly men, but in reality you're speaking to a woman on the other end of the phone. that is because you're talking to the person who has the responsibility in the family to guide on a treatment pathway.

Psychographics also comes into play. We might ask, "How do you think you approach things? Are you analytical? Are you more social? Are you collaborative?" If we can understand how a prospective patient approaches life, we are able to paint a picture with our words and questions of how a consumer might interact with brands or providers.

In our health and risk assessment quizzes, a psychographic profile can emerge. We ask these profiling questions not because we're trying to dig in or invade someone's privacy, but to understand how to speak to them with the right tone. Everyone has a way they prefer information conveyed to them. Speaking at "tone" assures that your message is being heard, consumed, and understood.

There are four distinct personality types:

- The results-oriented person who prefers information to be short versed, very direct and blunt without a lot of flowery language. That person has a specific need. They like to have concise, condensed information given to them very quickly.

- The analytical person who wants to know facts and numbers. They want to make decisions based on data.

- The highly cooperative person who does not like conflict and won't get in a confrontation. They will be passive on the phone. They require continuous check-ins to make sure that they're okay and that they get all the information they need.

- The socially oriented person who is interested in testimonials and who else has used the service.

We may be delivering the same information, it may be 85% the same in facts, but the delivery methodology accounts for that last 15% which determines whether the person really hears it.

We constantly talk about speaking with tone, because if you're speaking with a lot of numbers to someone who relies on testimonials and wants to hear other people's experiences and doesn't really care about numbers, you've really not helped that person. We're not in the business of doing all this work to not help people. We also realize that someone's health care status is very serious business. We, in essence, are the bridge to hope for distraught and frustrated prospective patients on the other end of the phone.

Given all these demographic and psychographic insights, you can literally draw a picture of your target health care consumer. This is the persona you can serve by delivering the patient activation process.

Measurable behavior change

In recent years, the Patient Activation Measure-13 (PAM-13) has come to play a major role in assessing a person's ability to engage with his or her health behavior.

Patient activation measurement specifies the level of a patient's engagement and may contribute to better self-management, higher engagement in treatment, and greater patient satisfaction. In addition, patient activation is associated with better health outcomes.

The Patient Activation Measure-13 (PAM-13), developed by Hibbard et al., ascertains health engagement and thereby self-reported knowledge, skills, behaviors, and confidence for self-management of health and chronic diseases.

Previous research has mostly examined patient activation among adults with chronic conditions and in primary care settings. There are a few examples of addressing patient activation considerations in developing disease awareness campaigns, marketing promotions, educational outreach, compliance programs, or clinical trial recruitment.

83bar has developed a patient activation system that has been implemented by some 50 name brands in health, medical, technology, and devices. The company has a database of more than 850,000 patient prospects over the past three years.

The validation of PAM principles has been examined across adults with chronic conditions, among multimorbid older adults, in surgical settings, in neurological populations, among people with diabetes, on patients with fibromyalgia, in a primary care setting, and for patients with rare disease conditions.

The Patient Activation Measure is a tool that helps to measure the spectrum of skills and confidence in patients, and then captures the extent to which people feel engaged in taking care of their condition. Individuals complete a short survey, rating their degree of agreement with the following statements:

1. When all is said and done, I am the person who is responsible for managing my health condition.

2. Taking an active role in my own health care is the most important factor in determining my health and ability to function.

3. I am confident that I can take actions that will help prevent or minimize some symptoms or problems associated with my health condition.

4. I know what each of my prescribed medications does.

5. I am confident I can tell when I need to go get medical care and when I can handle a health problem myself.

6. I am confident I can tell my health provider the concerns I have even when he or she does not ask.

7. I am confident I can follow through on the medical treatment I need to do at home.

8. I understand the nature and causes of my health condition.

9. I know the different medical treatment options available for my health condition.

10. I have been able to maintain the lifestyle changes I have made for my health.

11. I know how to prevent further problems with my health condition.

12. I am confident I can find a solution when new situations or problems arise with my health condition.

13. I am confident I can maintain lifestyle changes, like diet and exercise, even during times of stress.

Assessing activation in an early stage can be useful when planning the targeting and messaging to understand how patients engage in their own health.

Prototypical Patient: Susan's Prognosis

Watching her daughter Laura smile and laugh while she and her new husband cut the cake, Susan Suvida remembered her own wedding day, thirty-five years before. Her grandmother had hugged her delicately, as though she were a precious flower standing in the sunlight slanting through the stained glass window. Bestowing her blessing like a prophecy, Carmen had firmly said: "May you be blessed with many children as lovely and loving as mine."

Grandmother's blessing had come true; Susan and Anthony had been blessed with five beautiful, healthy children. Today her youngest was marrying a young man who was kind, generous, and ambitious; she felt blessed beyond measure.

Yet she grew increasingly uncomfortable. She had needed to go to the restroom ever since the young couple had said, "I do," but the celebrating that had begun immediately afterward and the hugs and greetings and well-wishes from family and friends had kept Susan in the sanctuary. Then one of the nieces had rushed in, panicking because she needed help with last-minute adjustments to the cake before the reception could start, so Susan had scooted off to the kitchen to help finalize the preparations. As she was finishing that, the photographer announced that he needed the bride's family to immediately meet once again out on the lawn for a few quick retakes—before the approaching rainstorm could shed its crystal confetti—because a stray cat had wandered into the frame, previously unseen in the background, and ruined the shots taken before the ceremony.

By this time Susan needed to go to the restroom desperately but the one nearest to the fellowship hall where they were having the reception was out of order; the only restroom in working order was all the way down a series of long halls on the other side of the sanctuary. Did she have time to run all the way over there and get back before they started shooting? What if there was a line again, as there had been before the ceremony? She hated to insist upon using it first, making others wait. She would almost rather wet herself than be rude, and she also hated the idea of making the photographer and everyone else wait. So she squirmed, wondering whether she could hold it.

She didn't worry much when she first noticed that she was having to go to the restroom often; she thought at first that she had just been drinking too much soda, tea, or water (though she knew in her heart that wasn't so) and then she had thought she just needed to exercise more. Finally, after months and months of swim aerobics and getting into the habit of taking daily evening walks with her little dog, Manny, she found that she was still frequently having to go. Sometimes, she didn't actually have to go; it just felt like she did.

That was even more frustrating because at times it caused her to panic. It was terribly inconvenient, for example, when the urge suddenly ambushed her while she was waiting in the line in the grocery store or at the pharmacy. She was sometimes angry at herself for not going earlier (but she had not had to go!) as she was forced to push her cart hurriedly down the aisles, trying not to run over other people.

Other times she had been forced to park at the school and run into the building while picking up her grandchildren from school, instead of waiting in the carpool line. She felt terrible when she had to tug their little hands through school hallways or at the baseball field, trying to get them to walk faster as she squeezed with all her might to keep from having another accident, only to end up having nothing or very little come out.

Susan couldn't remember whether her mother, her aunts, or her grandmother had ever talked about having this problem. Finally, she decided her little "accidents" and frequent need to urinate were just a natural part of aging. She hadn't worried too much these last two years that she had been feeling this way because she was almost always able to find and use a restroom quickly, wherever she went. But lately she had been forced to get up to go to the restroom two or three times in the night. This was getting to be too much! And situations like today really bothered her; she hated worrying about such a thing on a day when she should be enjoying each moment fully!

Well, she didn't have time to worry about it now. She decided when everything had quieted down and everyone had gone home, she would do some research, find out what was causing her to have this trouble and what she could do about it. She had overcome health problems before, and she was confident she could do it again. Like her mother and her grandmother, she was practical, a realist but also hopeful. On occasions such as this, though, when all of the family had gathered to celebrate such a lovely occasion, Susan wished with all her heart that she did not have to struggle with this, this… whatever it was. This condition.

Later that evening, Susan went to Google her symptoms, paper and pen ready, and felt a little relief right away when she learned that she may just have an overactive bladder. She jotted down the symptoms that pertained to her—difficulty emptying her bladder, a strong urge to urinate, and loss of bladder control—and was thankful that she didn't have the others: blood in her urine, red or dark brown urine, painful urination, pain in her side or groin, or fever.

Feeling much better that she was not experiencing anything terribly uncommon, Susan studied about a dozen articles—taking notes all the while—then drove to the pharmacy to see if she could find some medicine that would work. She bought something with oxybutynin and felt more hopeful than she had felt in a long time.

Chapter 2:

The Difference Between Awareness and ACTIVATION

Patients can often feel bewildered by the amount of choices, complexity, and information. The gap between a passive patient and an informed health care consumer is having curated resources that can help them digest the information, understand the complexity, and make informed decisions.

Basically, success is all about closing the gap between awareness and action. That process is called patient activation because it results in a health care consumer who is ready to make an informed decision, take control of their health, and get on the path to wellness.

It sounds so simple. Yet it challenges the best in the industry.

Even the Chief Experience Officer of the Cleveland Clinic (who is also a staff neurologist) expressed the difficulty in focusing when she wrote,

"The field of patient experience has exploded. At the same time, as population health efforts multiply, efforts to engage patients in their own health have become very popular. Yet these two concepts seem disconnected. Health care professionals talk about engagement in health, but not always the experience of it. We talk about the experience of our patients, but not always their engagement. So . . . what are we really talking about? Do we even know?

"To further thicken the plot, technology vendors have leapt into the engagement space and are designing many intelligent, empathic solutions to drive engagement and experience. Yet, in a recent conversation with the CEO of an engagement technology company, I asked how he measures patient engagement. His response: 'number of downloads or clicks.' I felt pretty sure that the academic community would find that inadequate. Download frequency may be a helpful metric for engaging people in technology, but not necessarily their health."

That is why I felt compelled to take a fundamentally different approach—to create a fully integrated patient activation system. This awareness-to-action process results in more prospects who are prepared and motivated to act, and then qualified for referral.

The difference starts with acknowledging that activation may start with "awareness," but it emphatically does not end there.

Dr. Ezekiel Emanuel alludes to this in his recent book, *Prescription for the Future*. Dr. Emanuel is the vice provost and chair of the Department of Medical Ethics and Health Policy at the University of Pennsylvania. He asks:

"Will the latest computer-based technologies like apps, wearables, remote monitors, and other high-tech devices make Americans healthier? After all, as behavioral economists remind us, information alone doesn't change behavior.

"Smokers know that smoking is bad for them and that they should quit. Obese people know that they should lose weight. People want to take their medications and do their rehabilitation exercises, but all of this requires altering habits and daily routines, which is supremely difficult."

So, he says, if it all sounds too good to be true, that is because it is. Computer-enabled technology can indeed change the practice of medicine, but it must augment traditional care, not simply catalyze a medical revolution prophesied by Silicon Valley.

Rather than machine learning or remote observations of monitoring technology, our patient activation process is a technology-driven communication system that involves changing patients' habits and behaviors once they recognize a health problem and feel motivated to change it.

Specifically, 83bar system is supported by technology in all four steps of the process:

- locate

- educate

- navigate

- advocate

What Dr. Emanuel supports, and we have documented, is that the only interventions that seem to change the behavior of patients in a lasting way are those that involve structured, person-to-person relationships with nurses and health care coordinators. These interventions are high-touch-driven and enabled by high-tech.

They remain our most effective prescriptions to treat chronic illnesses.

Beyond traditional DTC advertising

This difference is all the more interesting when you think of the millions and millions of dollars spent on direct-to-consumer (DTC) advertising by pharma companies, device manufacturers, diagnostic businesses, and more.

Let's look back at the assumptions of the past that informed this strategy.

The prevailing model for the last fifty years on the medical side was driven by sales and marketing. Up until the 1980's, it was one-directional. A company hired sales reps who went into doctors' offices, and those doctors were the gatekeepers who controlled all of the recommendations and referrals to patients. Therefore, if a company had a product, service, or diagnostic to sell, that is the way it was sold.

That changed in the 1980s when Pfizer launched Viagra into the marketplace and people were driven by consumer advertising to go in and actually ask the doctor about a product. Pfizer created awareness which prompted consumers to do something.

It worked great for so-called "lifestyle" pharmaceuticals like Viagra where the cause and effect was pretty evident and was outside the normal traditional model of a reimbursed-type of drug. This route became the basis for DTC advertising, but it has never really progressed much beyond that.

Much of the DTC advertising since then has just continually created more awareness. The problem with this kind of awareness for physician offices is that everybody comes in looking for the drug they saw on TV. They go in to talk to their physician about it, but they really don't have an idea what it does. They don't understand any of the side effects. All they know is "Hey, I saw this on TV," and the physician is forced to have the same conversation over and over again. Quite frankly, they get annoyed. Doctors in general get annoyed at having to become the order fulfillment house for pharma and diagnostic companies.

This strategy hasn't improved with time. There was an early attempt in the 1990s and 2000s by American Healthways and several other patient case management companies who tried to manage patients. But they were typically post-intervention, so when someone was diagnosed, the company managed her post-intervention and tried to keep her out of the doctor's office on a routine basis. However, that didn't work well because the compliance ratio was fairly low, and there wasn't any true economic model to reward anyone.

So, here we sit. It's 2019, and the system in place is still broken. The patient wants to get better, but she doesn't have the ability to get the right information. The doctor wants to be a good doctor, but he can't afford to be a walking billboard for 27 different pharmaceutical and diagnostic companies.

Ultimately, manufacturers are stuck trying to "get the word out" and the only way they can do it is by going directly to the consumer. The process is counterintuitive, for it creates more uncompensated work for the ones who are actually writing orders for companies' products. that is why it doesn't work and why it's so hard and very expensive to get these innovative services to market. It's quite a quandary.

Ripe market for a different approach

Health care is different because education and a conversation about health care is one, very personal, and two, very technically complex. As a health care operator myself, I always treated our "consumers" as patients. But I finally was compelled to turn those patients into consumers.

The reason that we treated them like patients in the past is because we didn't understand that we were simply creating a state of awareness without a complete map to a decision point.

Let me explain:

The health care ecosystem is composed of innovative people coming up with novel medicines, devices, and diagnostic tools with very complex science. They shout at patients, "Here I am! Look what I'm doing. This could help you." There are thousands of these encounters and messages; it is difficult for doctors and patients to digest.

Contrast that ecosystem with the technology-based communication platform that can be completely decentralized to have those health conversations where a patient feels most comfortable— in their home, in their backyard, on their couch. She is in a place where she can be open and honest with a clinician on the other end of the phone who is educating and navigating her through the medical delivery system.

Just as important, the process has to be completely integrated. From locating that patient early on in her discovery journey to educating and navigating her through the entire process all the way to scheduling appointments for her. Then, on the back end, making sure that everything goes according to plan and arming her with tools to tell her story.

For the first time, innovators and 83bar business partners have a method for holding service providers and their partners accountable. We have measurable metrics. We can track exactly what's going on at all times. It's not throwing money out and hoping to get something back. It's spending $1.00 and getting $7.57 in return, down to that level of detail. that is really what we're talking about here.

Are you starting to see the difference? Patient activation is delivered on a technology-driven concierge platform, to help turn passive patients into active consumers of health care. That means we help patients accelerate their path to wellness.

The patient experience: The Gents Place and the origin of 83bar

Let me illustrate the difference with a story from another market, with which you'll see the difference between a regular men's haircut and a concierge service for men's personal grooming and wellness needs. You will also see creating a pathway from a consumer to move from a state of awareness to a state of activation.

I went for a haircut one day into this new place in the neighborhood called The Gents Place. It was pretty upscale, and the price of a haircut was about $40. As soon as I walked in, I noticed it didn't look like any other barbershop.

It had wood paneling. The guy behind the desk offered me a drink and then paid me a lot of personal attention. I went with one of the stylists, who was very nice to me. I took particular notice of the person running it, Ben Davis. He was a young guy, very attentive, and he was sweeping the floors. He made sure all the details were in their proper place.

We started having a conversation.

He had borrowed about as much money as he could; this was in 2008. Obviously it was the depth of the recession, and he was trying to sell a very premium product. He was struggling, and having a tough go of it. The business was doing $15,000-20,000 a month, but wasn't making any headway. He was trying to figure out what the next steps were, and what would make the business work.

My first point to him was simple: You've got a good thing going here, you only have so much money left, and you need to make it work. He agreed with me, and my second point to him was, if people come in and they have the experience, do they like it? He said, "Yeah, everybody I can get in the door likes it, but my price point makes it hard to compete with Sports Clips and all the others that are available."

The Gents Place is a grooming and wellness business that provides a very high level of concierge service for men. In particular, it delivers service for haircuts, pedicures, manicures, and those type of things, but not in the traditional sense. It really sells a confidence experience. What a confidence experience means is that, if we make you feel more confident in yourself, you go into the world as a more confident man— and as a more confident man you will be more successful.

What is interesting is the average haircut at The Gents Place now runs about $55 for an entry level, all the way up to about $100 for a master level.

No man would pay that type of money for a normal haircut, especially when he might be getting one cut every three or four weeks. It's just not the way men think, and so to change the business model and turn it into a subscription model, it had to be focused on an experience. Here's the story about how that got started, and about our partnership, and how we created the system.

I can still remember the defining moment when we said, "Well, let's just give it away, because if we're so sure the product is that good and we're so sure the experience is that good, then let's make the bet on ourselves. Instead of spending money, let's just give the product away but think of it as an experience test drive." It was the beginning of the formation of the experience model, rather than the product-function model.

Over the next couple of weeks, we worked on a sales plan that would do just that. We started advertising free appointments, with available upgrades, much the same as we have done for consults in the medical model. Soon we were climbing into the $40,000 and $50,000-a-month range. The place got profitable, and the story continues. It's now a subscription model that is going national with multiple locations.

Emmitt Smith, former running back star for the Dallas Cowboys, is now his partner, along with Jerry Jones, owner of the Cowboys. They're selling franchises throughout the country. The same core ideas still guide us: "We're so good at what we do, that we're willing to bet our own money" to give you that experience for a free test drive. We are that confident.

The "test-drive experience" is a highly orchestrated, very well thought out, extraordinarily personalized sales experience that allows the person to engage on their own timeline and experience it in their own way. They are provided with the ability to personalize a program built around their individual needs, whether they get their hair cut two times a month, three times a month, or four times a month.

Again, the focus is not on merely providing services but on instilling confidence in the men who come into the business; the success of the endeavor is perceived by the individual through the lens of their own unique experience.

In essence, you have removed the friction in the transaction so it makes it easy to go from a state of awareness to a state of activation (subscriber). Although the model has medical roots, it has worked in a consumer model just as well.

It is thinking about what you're going to do for someone else, or thinking about building something to give to someone else in exchange for something. Now, oftentimes the best businesses are when you're doing something that is exponentially better for somebody, to the point where they feel like they can't live without it, e.g. Apple, and so forth.

For the most part, business owners think of their offering in a two-dimensional mode—product and services—and how those two are associated. If we think about this in a three-dimensional way, we will think about the experience the person wants to have. Then the service and the products become somewhat of the experience filler, or the matrix that makes up the experience. You will tend to build a model that people will become much more emotionally attached to, and the gratification level will be much more deeply implanted. You will have a much more valuable client/customer relationship going forward.

Most of all, do not assume that the prospective patient/consumer understands how to move from just being aware of your business to being actively involved. Your patients are counting on you to show them the way from awareness to activation.

A different approach for a medical device in a clinical trial

We executed a plan using our patient activation system for a major device company to accelerate enrollment in a global clinical trial in a hard-to-treat cardiovascular disease.

The goal of this campaign was both to increase enrollment in the clinical trial and to make qualifying new study candidates simple. We launched the campaign, following IRB (institutional review board) approval, and initially focused on one arm of the study.

How did the campaign work? We went directly to the consumer with an online lead-generation campaign that attracted, qualified, and then navigated candidates to a phone consultation with the study site coordinator.

- We served ads on Facebook, Google, local radio, and print to attract interest.

- We used a quiz to spark interest and to pre-qualify candidates for eligibility.

- We responded very quickly, usually within minutes, with nurses who have a high degree of experience. These nurses educated, qualified, and screened candidates.

- Candidates were transferred to the site coordinator.

- We then sent emails and texts to ensure the candidate followed through with their phone consultation.

Now you may be wondering, what exactly could our nurses screen for over the phone? Through both our online quiz and nurse outreach, we were collecting most of the information sites need to determine eligibility for this trial based on the study's inclusion and exclusion criteria. All of this information was then documented in our HIPAA compliant dashboard. If a candidate did not meet an obvious eligibility requirement, they were not passed on to the clinic, saving the coordinator's time.

How were these candidates transferred to the site? If it was during office hours and they told us they were available to take calls, our nurses called directly and transferred the candidate over the phone. If it was after office hours or they were not available to take a call, we scheduled the candidate via a shared calendar for a time that was most convenient for them and also for the clinic. Such flexibility works best for everyone.

The clinical trial sites really liked partnership. Once we transferred a candidate to them, they helped confirm eligibility and interest, ensuring the candidate was ready to move forward. Patients had questions that only site coordinators could answer. They needed to schedule their first in-office visit. Most important, we needed them to update the 83bar dashboard in order to optimize this campaign. We needed just five minutes from them every week, to let us know what happened to the candidates that we sent their way.

Anyone on the front line of health care delivery will tell you they are more efficient with patients who are educated and prepared to act (in the state of pre-activation) in contrast to patients who are vaguely aware of their condition or why they are even in the clinical trial pathway (state of awareness).

Activated patients for market research

Starting in 2016, we created an outreach campaign for focus groups and advisory boards involving patients with a rare condition called Eosinophilic Esophagitis.

Eosinophilic Esophagitis (EoE) is a chronic, immune- mediated disease characterized by the presence of tissue eosinophilia and symptoms of esophageal dysfunction. To date, no medications have been FDA-approved to treat this condition. A mid-size pharma company developed a novel tablet containing a proven active pharmaceutical ingredient.

Patient market research is an integral part of the pre-launch process. Along with clinical insights, patient insights guide the education and communication initiatives.

We created the outreach effort under the theme, "My EOE Story," which conveyed shared experiences in a very personal voice. Our social media campaign promoted that patients could help support clinical development to advance treatment for EOE. Specifically, the word "development" was more motivating than "research" or "studies" because it connoted progress.

Summary: From Awareness to Action

We would all be better served to re-think our products and services, especially when thinking about health care, because health care is deeply personal. Too often in the past, patients were delivered care in terms of selling a product, ordering a test, doing a procedure, and billing for time.

Going forward, let's think about what that person is going through at that moment (they are probably not wondering how to "ask my doctor if this is right for me.") In the past, treatment was more of a production line, not empathizing with how a person is engaging with their health care. But the wake-up call has come.

Awareness alone may have worked ten or twenty years ago, when a doctor may have just told the patient what to do and hoped they did it. But it's not working now, and it will not work five years from now.

It's time for us to adapt or die. And the way to adapt is to look at patient activation from an experiential point of view.

Prototypical Patient: Susan's Privilege — Activated and Confident

Anthony came into the bedroom and found Susan crying softly. This shocked him because she rarely ever cried; in all the years they had been married he could only remember her crying a handful of times.

Sitting on the bed, he embraced her. "What is wrong, mi alma?"

Strengthened by his calm compassion as always, Susan wiped her tears. "I've been taking the medicine I bought at CVS drugstore but it just isn't helping." She had done more research in the several months since she had learned she had an overactive bladder, but nothing suggested online was helping her. She had been taking her medicine faithfully as well as doing some exercises to strengthen her pelvic floor muscles, but her condition had not improved. In fact, it had only gotten worse.

Aware that others in her family might have suffered from the same symptoms, she had finally asked her aunt and a cousin whether they knew about the condition and what to do. She had confessed humbly to her aunt, "I have to use Depends now."

Nodding, Aunt Celeste had empathized. "They're expensive."

"Yes, even though I use every coupon I can find."

Her cousin had told her, "The medicine I got from my doctor only helped me a little bit for a couple months, and I had to keep going back for other appointments. The doctor visits and the medicine were so expensive! It has just not been worth it."

So Susan had not made an appointment for herself; she just couldn't afford it. But it had gotten to the point where she hated going anywhere. It was just easier to stay home, where she could run to the restroom as many times as she needed without having accidents. The anxiety and being so confined had taken their toll; Susan was miserable.

Anthony comforted his wife and told her to look for a clinic that may be able to help her; he would work overtime and on the weekends to pay for her visit and whatever medicine they prescribed. When he wouldn't take "No" for an answer, she thanked him with a hug and a kiss and went immediately to the computer.

While searching on Google, Susan saw a banner which contained exactly what she was looking for. It read, "Find Overactive Bladder Treatment | Restore My Control." Her curiosity grew when she saw that it said, "Find out if advanced overactive bladder treatment options can help you by taking our 1-minute quiz." She thought it wouldn't hurt to take the quiz and see if she could learn something new.

The name of the website, RESTOREMYCONTROL.COM, promised Susan exactly what she needed and the offer to "work with a recognized bladder specialist for a personalized treatment plan that can help bring lasting relief" almost made her cry again with the thought of enjoying life again. A little worry crept in with the thought that a bladder specialist must be very expensive, but she decided she would do everything she could to not only fix her problem but also learn as much as possible so that she could share her knowledge with her family members who were suffering from the same condition.

She finished the quiz within a few minutes, for it had just eight simple questions; they asked her gender, age, symptoms, medications, satisfaction with current treatment, interest in new alternatives, and contact details. She finished by giving her consent to be called by a registered nurse.

Five minutes later Susan's phone rang and a woman introduced herself. "My name is Margaret but you can call me Meg," the woman said. Her tone was friendly and professional. She explained that she had been a registered nurse for over twenty-five years. She would carefully go over the answers Susan had given to the "Restore My Control Quiz," then she would help Susan understand the treatment options available as well as answer any and all questions Susan had.

As she spoke to Meg and received answers to her first questions, Susan's relief shone on her face. She grew more and more confident that she had finally found the solution she had been searching for. Anthony felt relief, too, when he came into the room and saw his wife smiling for the first time in a long time.

We've already established that consumers are looking for better ways to take responsibility for the cost of their health care. The number of self-managed health care consumers is rising as a result of rising deductibles, rising co-pays, and rising premiums.

PART II:

THE 4-PART SYSTEM OF PATIENT ACTIVATION

Chapter 3:

Step 1 = Locate

We also know that consumers consider digital solutions as the most effective way to meet their health care needs. A survey showed the percentage of patients who prefer digital solutions to the following health care needs:

- 81% shop for a health plan

- 82% check health information

- 85% pay bills

- 84% search frequently for a doctor

- 82% monitor health metrics

- 79% purchase insurance

In short, today's health care consumer uses digital tools to find health care solutions. But who's looking out for the patients and who's looking to find them? This is where the 83bar process comes in and the first step is to locate patients.

Pinpoint patients early in their search

In the identification step, we find patients who say, "I don't feel right. Something worries me. I've got questions." Our methods are designed to pinpoint prospective patients early in their search.

In this first step, we create a coordinated campaign of social media, landing pages, symptom assessment, and data collection. While it may seem that there are multiple hurdles or steps to gaining this information, these micro-commitments actually help demonstrate a high level of intent by the patient.

In order to progress from being attracted by the product proposition to engaging with educational information, we move them through a communication flow. Some of the questions we anticipate are:

- What symptoms are important for me to highlight?

- What should I track before my appointment?

- Who's the best at treating this condition?

- What are my options?

- Who takes my insurance?

- How should I organize my thoughts before discussing them with the doctor?

- Who can I trust?

- What happens next?

By creating a coordinated communications campaign, we help patients understand what options are available and what to discuss. They would already have a hierarchy of symptoms ready for the doctor and a game plan for their visit.

The kind of information we use to target patients is also captured in a full-circle data collection approach. This includes gender, age, symptoms, medications, satisfaction with current treatment, interest in new alternatives, and contact details.

Factors of a creative campaign

When developing a social media ad campaign, we try to ensure that it will connect, that it's honest, easy to understand, and motivating. We found that a combination of relevant lifestyle graphics with captivating medical illustrations can be most attention-getting. The creative campaign is designed to also connect with target prospects emotionally. The call to action is for prospects to self-select into the funnel by clicking "Learn More." Most social media advertising platforms, like Facebook, have an algorithm that helps us create the best-performing ads that build credibility and stand out from the crowd.

Next, our technique of the health assessment quiz uses micro-commitments and gamified data collection to yield high conversion percentages while providing an absolute value exchange. The process works like this: prospective patients searching for health information on Facebook or Google find our sponsored quiz. This is a health risk assessment in the form of a survey. They begin to engage the questionnaire. The questionnaire is typically six to ten questions long. It asks a series of well-researched questions about what's important to them and what they're trying to get accomplished.

It may seem there is a bit of black magic in the structure of the question set. There is a need to find a balance: There must be introspective questions that imply value to the taker as well as disclosing questions that will assist the Nurse Educator to actually help the prospective patient in their search.

Please note that our thesis of eight-plus questions directly contradicts the industry practice of "Ask as few questions as possible and grab the prospect's contact information." In this vein, we never once believed we were in the lead generation business, as no one in their right mind would put so many hurdles (question steps) between a click from an ad and a form submission.

Rather, we have always viewed ourselves as sherpas, providing valuable (sometimes lifesaving) advice and support on their way back to well. Part of that process is making sure both parties are committed to success; hence, our comprehensive intake approach to our education and navigation process. Remember, we are ultimately responsible for preparing the patient for a state of "activation," so this is our homework phase.

Once that question set is completed, our prospective patients give us permission to call them and talk to them. They are informed that the next step is going to be a registered nurse reaching out to them to carefully review their answers to the question set. This will help them begin their health care journey.

In the context of HIPAA guidelines and the new GDPR regulations in Europe, controversies and power struggles over data have increased in intensity. Consumer data is rapidly becoming the dominant currency of the modern health care marketplace. In fact, recent IAB research credits first-party data as the driver for all significant functions of an enterprise, such as product development, customer value analysis, and pricing. It's impossible to achieve the critical goals the market now demands—empathy, fluid conversation across touchpoints, and personalization—without the nimble, proficient command of consumer data. It will be interesting to see how this all pans out.

Whose data is it anyway?

In today's digital world, data is the source of performance advantage; specifically first-party data, which is the information that a brand or company collects about its customers through digital interactions. First-party or customer marketing data is available to companies at no cost and is widely considered to be the most relevant and accurate information that can be gathered because it comes directly from the source. Access to this data offers unprecedented insight into customers' behaviors, attitudes, and motivations, enabling new levels of personalization, optimization, and ultimately trust.

But many marketers find themselves in a situation of not having access to primary data, and therefore, cannot use it, control it, or develop it over time. They miss out on the ability to build a sound data-based strategy.

As the ad technology landscape expanded, marketers turned to providers to help them navigate the complex ecosystem, and in the process lost control and ownership of their own data.

In the proprietary systems we've built, we help clients not only maintain control and access of the data, but also help maximize its potential. Our refrain: "Click, capture, and qualify."

- CLICK: Develop and optimize online ads that work. Because of our exclusive focus on treatments, diagnostics, and devices, we have learned what prompts health care consumers to click through. Plus, perpetual testing and optimization have helped us often double the lead flow of a client's previous campaigns and drive down leads costs by as much as 80%.

- CAPTURE: Create landing pages, surveys, and quizzes that capture interest, capturing leads with robust data collection fields and functional reporting. All detailed demographic information on leads and patients is collected and saved in HIPAA-compliant ways. Most of all, the data on ROI and performance is completely transparent to the clients. After the initial campaign launch, the optimization process tracks multiple metrics on a daily basis (cost per lead, click-thru rate, contact rate, hand off/booking rate, sales rate, drop offs) and are used to continuously refine the funnel.

- QUALIFY: Utilize a distributed network of nurses to return patient inquiries in less than five minutes, a different organization, consisting of a call center staffed by registered nurses who educate and qualify leads before they schedule a doctor visit. It is designed for rapid response because we want to connect with prospective patients while symptoms and concerns are top-of-mind.

Why it is relevant to get "personal"

Looking ahead, Accenture Interactive's Personalization Pulse report says, "Consumers are more likely to shop at the brand that treats them in a personalized manner." The survey shows that 91% of consumers are more likely to shop with brands they recognize and remember, and those that provide them with relevant offers and recommendations.

Surprisingly, rather than being wary of surrendering their data, consumers want increased levels of personalization. The report finds consumers are willing to share their data and rarely feel that companies are too personal. They want to see proof that you're getting to know them even more personally as time goes by. Nearly three-quarters of consumers say that no retailers or service provider has ever communicated with them in a way that they felt was too personalized. In fact, failure to leverage data to create great experiences comes with a warning. Nearly half of respondents said they have left a business' website and made a purchase elsewhere because the experience was poorly curated.

In addition to the personal data consumers are willing to share, there's another kind of data emerging, and that is self-reported data on compliance and health care habits being collected from connected devices such as smartphones, fitness trackers, and digital diaries. These contain a portrait of the patient in their own environment without the edited version of health many patients recollect and report during physician visits.

As a professional engaged in the field of marketing, it is very important to find the balance in your duties and loyalties. You are paid to help your employer spread the message. Oftentimes, the requests for help in health care come from consumers.

At 83bar, we take the position that our focus is the consumer (prospective patient). If we do our job well, that prospective patient becomes an actual patient and the unit economics take care of themselves.

We make our purpose and our intent very clear. We make prospective patients jump through multiple hurdles to engage us to make sure we are not bothering anyone who is not truly interested and committed. Once the request is made, our efforts are monomaniacal toward getting that patient from a state of awareness to activation with the right intervention at the right time with the right provider.

In addition to data captured about the growing baby boomer population, mobile health solutions also make access to the physician more convenient via mobile telemedicine and video conferencing technologies. For many Americans, distant proximity to health care facilities creates a burden which may require several hours of transit and dependency on caregivers or public transportation. New inexpensive telemedicine techniques could lessen this challenge and provide more frequent and meaningful relationships with health care professionals.

Fit into their world; do not disrupt it

In the 83bar patient activation process, we're capturing consumers while they're doing their own online research. In this way, we're fitting into the health care world, not disrupting it. We have helped manufacturers and providers across many health care disciplines benefit from locating more patients in need. These include urologists, OB-GYNs, ENTs, neurologists, cardiologists, gastroenterologists, dentists, primary care physicians, and colorectal physicians.

Varied located patients

To be more specific, here are three examples of patient experiences, defined by clinical need, in which treatments began with locating the right patients.

- In overactive bladder, prospective patients are struggling with OAB symptoms with no positive corrective therapy in place. We located these patients by a custom bladder health assessment quiz. Then in our education step, we provided information around first, second, and third-line treatment options. In the navigation step, we were able to make a hand-off to office staff or even directly scheduled patients to see a physician. It might have taken weeks for them to make an appointment on their own.

- In genetic testing, prospective patients were considering BRCA genetic testing, usually at the suggestion of a close friend or because of a relative's cancer diagnosis. In locate, we used a clinically-driven hereditary cancer risk survey to identify potential prospects. Then we educated them about genetic testing, what it is and is not, benefits and insurance coverage, and how to think about the results. In navigation, a genetic counselor intervened when appropriate, followed by a hand-off or direct scheduling to see a provider.

- In IV hydration services, prospective patients struggle with ongoing relentless fatigue and are seeking high-concentration vitamin IV therapy. We were able to locate them by offering free, first IV-solution-based treatments. In the education phase, they were learning how an IV solution can help and how the clinic makes it easy and convenient. The navigation was to a self-scheduling tool to connect them with a clinic near them.

All of this discovery has been in contrast to what we refer to as "Dr. Google," meaning the constant internet searches that yield questionable results. It's also in contrast to referrals by family and friends who are well-meaning but often offer opinions based upon incomplete information.

Summary: First LOCATE Patients.

Once we have located patients in need, we can begin connecting these patients to the right provider. It has proven successful in all key segments of health care:

- In diagnostics, consumers do not understand why their genetics matter, nor do most doctors. Precision medicine is an inevitable solution as the market matures.

- In medical devices, technological advances are achieving market uptake in a very complicated pathway. Consumers' engagement from trial to consummation accelerates progress.

- For therapeutics, from clinical trial to medication compliance, patient education and navigation are key success drivers.

- In services, health care markets with declining service reimbursement revenues need better-prepared and ready-to-act patients to create more efficiency and better market penetration.

When the attraction net is turned on to LOCATE patients, our data capture starts and the clinical call center is ready to respond by contacting prospects. that is when real patient activation comes to life.

Prototypical Patient: Susan's Priorities

"I see you indicated the issues with which you have the greatest concern are 'Sudden or strong urge to urinate' and 'Leakage with little or no warning.'" Susan affirmed and Meg added, "These are the symptoms that most bother people with overactive bladder, so you are not alone in your frustration. Are these the only issues you're struggling with right now?"

Susan described the panic and embarrassment she had had at her daughter's wedding and recently in the grocery store. "I have basically stopped going anywhere unless I absolutely have to."

When Meg asked Susan how she had been managing her symptoms, Susan told her about all of the things she had been doing. "But nothing is really working" she ended, clearly worried.

Meg responded gently, with great care: "I understand how frustrated you must be. It must be terrible to miss out on so many activities with your family, especially your grandchildren." Susan believed the woman truly wanted to help her and felt reassured when Meg said firmly, "We can help you so that you won't have to suffer from overactive bladder any more."

"I'm ready to take control over my life again," Susan said.

"Great!" Meg replied. "What are you willing to do to have your freedom back?"

Chapter 4:

Step 2 = Educate

When we think about the role of education in the patient activation process, we don't think about it in the traditional sense. It is not a one-sided process in which we're the teacher and the prospective patient is the student.

Instead, envision it as a hybrid process in which we're both in the learning situation together. We're both trying to understand the patient's needs, and then we're both trying to provide some guidance. It is an education process that will enable both parties to make an informed decision and help each other make progress toward their respective goals.

Now, what do I mean by that?

The prospective patient comes into the process thinking that they might have a problem and they took the first step to fill out some sort of risk assessment (such as the online health surveys discussed in Chapter 1). When they press "submit," they've given us a detailed profile of what they're thinking about, what's in their head. And they have given us hints as to which direction we may be able to help them. However, it's not the full story. The full story is revealed as they talk to one of our nurses. The education process with one of our nurses is complex. It contains a series of steps which I will detail in this chapter.

Helping patients along their health care journey

Recapping step one of the process, a prospective patient found our health risk assessment survey while visiting a website, Facebook, or Google. It helps them reflect on several aspects of their health care questions and what they're searching to fix. As they engage in the questionnaire, typically six to ten questions long, their answers form a pattern that reveals what is important to them but at the same time, helps THEM to more clearly begin to articulate what they're trying to get accomplished.

Once that question set is done, we obtain permission to call and talk to them. They're clearly informed that in the next step, a registered nurse will reach out to them to review the question set and their answers. That consent is certainly a legal requirement in our business, but it's so much more. The patients WANT to talk with someone who can help them on their health care journey. It's reassuring to them that someone has offered to call. It's even more valued because a nurse is the single highest respected and trusted advisor status.

Response speed shows level of care

Within seconds of that form being submitted, the 83bar system reaches out to our network of nurses, much like the way a ride-sharing service pings its nearby drivers. The system dials one of our nurses, while it dials the patient at the same time.

The premise is that a prospective patient wants the answer right then and there. They don't want it the next day, and they certainly don't want to be talking about it at 2:00 in the afternoon in their office cubicle or at 3:00 in the afternoon when they're in a meeting and their phone is going off. We are making sure that when a patient is in the mindset to make a decision about their health care, we are there to serve them. This is our way to help them along the journey with the best possible service at the best possible time.

Change the system one educated patient at a time

Put this in the perspective of the big picture. If you want to make the whole US health care economy more efficient and more effective, you need to figure out how to get the patient to the right solution for the right intervention at the right time. In this way, you will get the best outcome.

This cannot be done by letting a patient bounce through the system like a ping-pong ball, trying one thing after another—a process known in the medical business, pejoratively, as "poke and hope."

Choices are everywhere, but the old process remains an inefficient, ineffective, and very costly health care system. In that system, patients continually go from one provider to the next, get redundant lab tests, duplicated diagnostic procedures, multiple diagnoses, and run up insurance bills while paying multiple co-pays and hitting their deductibles early every year.

I think we can create a better system. In fact, we have. We have created one where human intervention allows the provider to gather all the facts, organize the thoughts, provide a curated solution, and help the patient through the process. The whole process could be completed in one or two steps rather than ten or twelve.

Once we have become effective at doing this, we will have a better outcome-driven health care system in the United States that is more efficient and more effective. That is the mission, that is part of what we try to do in the educational process, and that is why it's important to intercede very quickly.

Patient activation provides the most educated and most informed patient up front; once informed, they are better able to make quality decisions. Knowing all available options gives them more confidence to commit to the right course of action.

Making sense of information overload

Answers to health-related questions of all kinds are of course available on the web; within milli-micro-seconds—as much time as it takes to move a mouse an inch—you have another answer. By the time you scroll three or four seconds, you probably have fifteen or twenty options. The problem is they are un-curated and unfiltered. You're searching at your own risk.

Now put yourself in the place of the person with a medical condition or a health question.

The prospective patient who doesn't know what they want and has limited medical knowledge is searching "Dr. Google." After typing in a few search terms, up comes hundreds (if not thousands) of potential answers and sources. Or maybe the same patient is on Facebook and they see all the different ads coming up about the issues they've been searching for.

Oftentimes that person has neither the educational wherewithal nor the life experience to navigate which is the best solution for them. How will they know the most appropriate solutions for their situation? The 83bar patient navigation system can be a guiding light.

In most families, when someone gets sick, there is always a person in the family who is the "nurse" or somehow medically connected. This person ends up being the go-to person, the one who serves as a translator for the family, guiding them through the medical process. that is what 83bar is in the telephonic world. The idea is we bring the nurse to the situation. Our nurses have an average of twenty years' experience and high levels of skill and empathy. Each nurse deploys that educational experience and life experience in interpreting what the patient has given us in the answers to the health assessment quiz. Thus equipped, the nurse can begin to help that patient through an education process in very quick manner.

Meeting the patient where she is

I've shared with you the importance of speed in responding to a patient in need. Now, I'd like to shift to another way to make the education step more effective: tone.

Why does tone make the process so much more effective? How do we actually hear as human beings when we discuss issues with each other?

First, over the course of our careers, many of us have been through personality type profiles, including Myers-Briggs, the DISC profile, or multiple others. The basic components come down to some level of four personality types. These four types influence behavior and are manifested in the population predictably. No matter which category you belong to, these tendencies seem to prevail and the message is still the same.

For clarity's sake, we'll use these definitions.

- A person who has a _social_ orientation is someone who is—and enjoys being—socially engaged often, likes the feedback loop of their friends and social circle, and hence actively seeks it out in their decision-making process.

- The person who has a _results_ orientation is oftentimes a very quick decision maker, seeks very little feedback outside of themselves and maybe a very close circle, tends to make decisions based upon perceived value, and usually has no regrets, unless it is not moving quickly enough.

- A prospect whose personality is oriented to be _cooperative_ is someone who tries to go along, to get along. They seek to have non-conflict in their lives. They typically are very difficult to understand when they say "Yes" because it is uncertain whether they really mean "Yes" or are only agreeing to avoid making a decision. (Out of the four prototypes, these are the most difficult to sell.)

- Finally, there is the _analytical_ personality type. That person typically relies on facts, figures, and numbers when making decisions. They're decidedly data driven. They don't really care about the number of testimonials you have from others; furthermore, they typically care little about what is said about a product because they're inherently skeptical or outright mistrustful and they want to do their own research.

Research shows that four general personality types are fairly evenly distributed in the population. We have experienced different successful education outcomes or conversion levels based on personality type. The patterns that emerged have helped us adapt and coordinate our strategies, for greater efficiency.

In our experience, we've had much more success with analytical and results-oriented personality types. In particular, when educating patients on lab testing—in which we are focused on moving numbers as a biomarker or some sort of chemistry profile, giving us the ability to gauge progress by a set of black and white numbers—the patients who respond best are those with an analytical mindset.

A results-oriented person responds when you have a very tight program. They know exactly what they're going to get and they know what kind of commitment it's going to take from their point of view. You'll get an even higher ratio of conversion when they realize you are saving them time.

Cooperatives can be very difficult to convince, but the most important thing to remember when working with cooperatives is that you must understand who they are so that you can decide whether you wish to continue to confirm their bias about whether they should move forward or not.

Finally, socially oriented personalities need many testimonials and a lot of content developed before you will be able to assist them in the decision-making process.

There are some of the highlights of a four-quadrant decision process and how it relates to getting a patient from being aware to being activated. To be clear, it relies upon making sure that you're speaking on tone. And tone can be nothing more than how a person hears through their perspective on life or their personality-influenced indexing.

Empathy is meaningful to the patient

Patient activation works because it revolves around an educated, experienced, and empathetic nurse. Nurses who score very high on an empathy scale use both clinical skills and their exceptional bedside manner to better serve the patient.

They review the question set that the prospective patient has already filled out to make sure there is a clear understanding of what that person is seeking. They are listening to what the patient wants to learn and how she is trying to make a decision, including what components she will need to help her make that decision.

After spending a few minutes reviewing what that person has completed on their survey, the process moves to the next portion, which is where the nurse uses her twenty years of experience as an RN to distill what the real issues are and begin to dig a little bit deeper in two-way conversation with the patient. Questions asked include:

- What is the issue you're struggling with right now?

- What do you want the outcome to be?

- What are you willing to do to create that desired outcome?

- What do you think the new normal needs to feel like?

- How much effort and time are you willing to put forward to obtain that right now?

Those are the types of questions that set up the education process and allow the nurse to begin a navigation process, (the step covered in the next chapter). The clear goal we have in mind is not met by a cookie-cutter approach; it is achieved by a highly personalized strategy, based on the prospective patient's needs, wants, and desires at this point.

Once that goal is established and the nurse begins to understand the deeper undertones of what someone's trying to accomplish, they begin an education process about the disease set, explaining what the disease or condition is and how it affects the patient, particularly in the long term. This is modified, of course, by how much that patient understands, which has been discerned by the early conversation with a patient. With a patient who's not very far in the learning curve, this takes a little longer; so we adjust on a per-patient basis.

When the patient has a full understanding and starts to feel comfortable that they understand, the nurse presents the potential options. Options typically might fit with what the patient has expressed about their desires, wishes, available time frames, and level of commitment. The difference is that now we can rank those options, guide the patient through an evaluation process, and enable them to make an informed decision.

At this point, the nurse typically does a check in and asks the patient, "Do you feel like this is going in the right direction? Is there something I'm missing? Is there anything else I could help you with?" The patient will typically try to reorient the conversation if they feel like it's not going in the correct direction. Now, once that is done, the patient has a sense of what they're dealing with and what the possible options are. The next questions aim for the navigation phase: "What would you like to do?" and "How can I help you take the next step?"

The education phase takes anywhere from three to ten minutes, depending on the starting point of the patient's knowledge curve and the applicable questions.

Depending on the situation, our education steps may include extended connections with patients. These might include messages to ensure attendance and encourage sustained interest with texts and reminders. Pre-appointment guides can be mailed, emailed, or texted to patients to maintain engagement and set expectations.

It doesn't have to take long because it's a structured, proven patient-centric communication process. The goal of this education discussion is for the patient to feel fully informed, comfortable, and prepared so that they can make an informed decision.

Activated patients are better for the provider, too

Our goal is relevant for the patient's health care provider who will be taking care of this prospective patient. She will be a better prepared patient who has fewer basic questions and is closer to making a decision by the time she arrives at the office.

Obviously, the goal for the manufacturer or the client who has engaged 83bar is to make sure that we're helping the right patient find the right solution in time to get the right outcome.

If this all works, everyone wins because the health care model is a much more efficient model when there is less friction, less bouncing. The quicker a patient goes from a point of concern to a point of resolution, the less money is spent, the less time is wasted, and the more gratified all parties are with the delivery model. that is why this education pillar is so important, so vital to making it work.

What we have learned

The first thing we've learned is that prospective patients have many demands upon their time and attention in this crazy, busy world we live in—as do we all.

The fact is if your medical practice company is not attentive and proactive to both inbound and outbound inquiries, you're setting yourself up for failure. We've learned this because we've tracked the dynamics and the interactions.

- About one third of the people who fill out the form actually talk to our nurse operators if we get to them within the first forty-five minutes after they have filled out the form.

- After three hours, the contact rate drops into the 20% range.

- Effectively, for every $100,000 you spend on marketing, you are giving away $40,000 to $45,000 based on the fact that you did not respond to people quickly enough.

This is primarily because of the way people now gather information on the web. There are just too many other opportunities; quite frankly, they may be looking for information about their health care issues one minute and the next minute they're looking at their checking account balance. The next thing you know, they're reading something else or watching CNN— and in the blink of an eye they're moving on with their life and they don't even remember what they were doing ten or fifteen minutes before.

The standard expectation of most companies is that if they call a prospect within a day or two, they are doing well. But I can't remember—no one can remember—what they were doing last night, forget about two days ago. People nowadays expect an instantaneous reaction and if they don't get it, they just move on to the next place or opportunity and whoever will give them that. that is why drive-thru windows and delivery and pick-up services are more popular and more profitable for restaurants than dining in. It boils down to today's lifestyle expectations.

Something else we've learned is "call one contact percentage." Ideally, you should not wait forty minutes; you really have to call within ten minutes if you want to get even one-third of those people to answer the phone. The reason is you are trying to occupy their attention space while they're sitting there after they've just typed in their inquiry or they've just clicked on an ad and actually filled the form out. Once they get up, your chances of reaching them diminish greatly; you can see the fallout over the course of minutes as it transcends from the transaction point.

Another thing we've found is that the person who is contacted quickly is three times more likely to book an appointment than if you reach her on the second, third, or fourth call. You read that right: THREE times more likely.

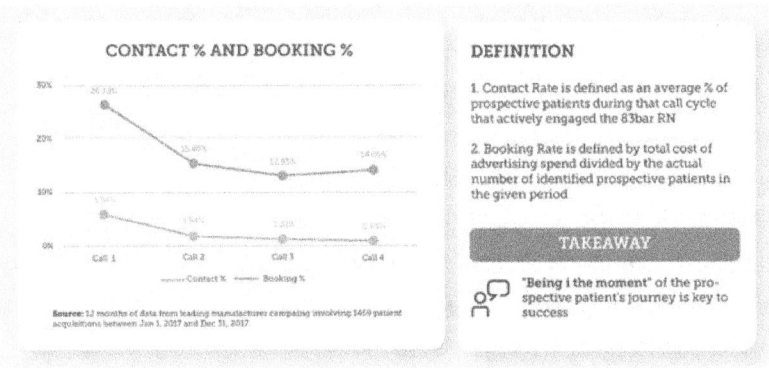

Let's think about that as a compounding factor. If it takes you two days to attempt to contact a prospective patient, you're only getting 15 to 20% of all of your leads that have come through. On top of that, if it's taking two to three phone calls to get them, you're only getting 20% of those 20% of leads.

How much is the compounding rate on that? That means you are taking $100,000 and only making about $20,000 of that effective. The system lacks the commitment of resources, time, and energy to be responsive. And we're not talking about fast food here. We're dealing with a patient who has said they need you. I can't stress enough how important that is.

We have also learned that this correlation is true even for complex medical circumstances. We worked with one of the industry's leading manufacturers of a very complicated, fourth-line type of treatment and surgical implant. The success rates were tied to the patients we got a hold of the quickest, who were helped to make a decision most quickly, and who booked with the doctors soonest.

If it takes you a long time to get in touch with prospective patients, your commitment rate is going to be a lot less than it is for people who are more assertive in the process.

Finally, one of the most important things we've learned is that you have key optimum points to turn that educational step into impact. You've got to get them on call one and you've got to get them as fast as we've discussed.

If they inbound call you, it is incredibly important to make sure that you answer that inbound call. In fact, our numbers argue that the callback from somebody for whom we left a message can actually close at a much higher rate than even the first call does. The second, third, and fourth call in a series produces a far less desirable result, so your system has to be built for speed and responsiveness, both inbound and outbound. If you do that, you'll be leagues ahead of your competitors. You have to think about speed in every one of the processes you build.

Finally, one mistake we made for a long time was thinking the conversation was one-to-one. It was never just one-to-one. We are talking to the patient, then the patient is going to talk to her family or friends, her social circle. Yet she left our call and might only remember two or three points. She can recall very little of what was said except for the highlights. That's why we started to create tools, mostly in print and downloadable PDF, which allow the patient to go home and communicate to a spouse. She can get family support behind her. Because if she is supported by the family, this patient will keep the appointment, come back for follow-up, adhere to the protocol, and so on.

For example, we suggest an optimal thyroid program for some of our clients. By providing a simple eight-page booklet guide, we helped people with hypothyroidism explain it to others. We proved we understand why they feel the way they do. This pushed us from a high 40% conversion rate to over 65%.

Summary: Educated Engagement

A patient today can bemoan the fact that they are only going to see the doctor for seven minutes or they can say, "I'm going to be an 'activated patient,' an empowered patient, an educated patient." More and more are choosing the latter.

That is what the 83bar process is all about: helping create and engage educated patients through our 4-part system. How are they better prepared to have that engagement with the doctor than they would have been otherwise?

I think it's all about being prepared to act. We focus on preparing patients so they're ready to act. They will be far better equipped to interact with you than average patients who come in with ads or printouts from their un-curated web research, what their friends have told them, or what they've heard. Activated patients waste far less time than those who waste the eight to ten minutes of a visit trying to go through a dissertation of scrambled facts without knowing how to organize their thoughts.

The 83bar methodology is completely different, because what we are effectively doing is preparing each patient to have all those questions answered beforehand by our nurses. And then equipping that patient to go in there prepared and ready to activate. Their questions are much more succinct and they also are of the mindset that they are there to engage and take the next step. They're not there to investigate, but to decide.

Prototypical Patient: Susan's Preparedness

Speaking with Meg about the symptoms, causes, and diagnosis of an overactive bladder, Susan lost her fear and grew confident that she would not have to settle for a life controlled by hers. She had felt trapped in her own home for many months, and she was ready to do whatever it takes to enjoy freedom again.

Meg assured her, "We will find a personalized treatment that works for you." As she reviewed first-line treatment options for OAB, Susan confirmed that she had already tried lifestyle and behavior modifications and several over-the-counter medications.

The next treatment step, Meg explained, involved visiting a physician who might recommend a prescription medication that would block the nerves controlling the bladder muscles.

"Are those medicines expensive?" Worry had crept back into Susan's voice, but Meg assured her there were affordable medicines for the condition. But, she added, some of those medications could have unwanted side effects. After listing some, Meg told Susan about the next line of OAB treatment options.

Advanced, third-line treatments include minimally invasive or surgical procedures such as sacral neuromodulation, tibial nerve stimulation, or bladder surgeries. Meg answered all of Susan's questions about each one and promised to email her several resources, including a PDF brochure with Q&A's, research data and statistics, and even detailed infographics about steps to take when you have chosen third-line therapy treatment.

She encouraged Susan to share the information with her husband; they should read the information together and think about what they would like to do. Finally, Meg scheduled a time two days later when she would call them to see if they had any questions and to learn whether they would like to follow through with taking the next step.

Chapter 5:

Step 3 = Navigate

In this chapter, I'll bridge the gap from the education pillar to the navigation pillar of the 83bar framework.

You can assume that once a prospective patient goes through the 83bar education process, they now have a baseline knowledge about their particular condition or disease state. We've reviewed all of their input and all of their assessment answers. We've identified their target desires, wishes, and goals for how they would like to proceed. And we've identified how much time and effort that they're willing to put forward, possibly even their financial ability to commit.

Once the patient has been fully prepared to make a decision and the patient says, "I'd really like to think about how to move forward and solve my issue," the navigation process can begin. The navigation process takes that patient from a thinking mode into an action mode. The active mode means making a commitment to a consultation, or beginning a process that would ultimately result in some sort of activation process in the medical delivery model.

The navigation process usually starts with more questions having to do with their financial ability to pay and insurance; some cost questions are often directed at that point, if applicable. Each pathway is tailored to individual needs. Oftentimes we begin to build a bridge by introducing multiple options that they have and ask them, "How would you like to make your decision?"

That is the bridge between education and navigation as we're moving patients through the process. Overall, we aim to make it easy, make it memorable, and make it personal.

We guide patients to action through service fulfillment or appointment scheduling, whichever is appropriate for the client.

We focus on action with clinically-appropriate innovation:

- Offer solutions

- Inform decision

- Provides 5-7 options in their area

- Offer scheduling (or info fulfillment)

- Appointment reminders + directions

We have applied our proprietary marketing automation processes to stay connected from the time of scheduling to the time of consult appointment. We have seen it work for a wide range of diseases, conditions, and medical specialties:

- Aesthetics

- Cardiology

- Diabetes

- Endocrinology

- Men's health

- Nutrition

- Oncology

- Ophthalmology

- Orthopedics

- Psychiatry

- Rare disease

- Surgery

- Urology

- Women's health

Surgery and surgery centers: We have clients who support a variety of procedures that can be done in surgery centers, such as sinus balloon surgeries, those type of procedures that can be done in an outpatient setting that are pretty disruptive to life on a day-to-day basis, but are not life-threatening. We have done a tremendous amount of work in the space focused on treating overactive bladder, bladder pain, and those types of things.

Aesthetics: We've worked with many female aesthetics providers, including those who offer vaginal rejuvenation and vaginal rebuilding, creating opportunities for people who are seeking those services. We've also worked with dermatologists who work not only on the sort of what I'll call the "clinical" side, the cancer side, but also provide aesthetic or quality-of-life improvement procedures and techniques.

Cardiology: We've worked with companies that provide cardiac implant products, as well as clinical trial recruitment for a hypertensive procedure.

Diabetes: We've had a long history in working with providers who treat diabetes. Early on, I cut my "business teeth" in the wound management service sector with the wound care centers, which really focused on diabetic wounds and vascular wounds. They did a tremendous amount of direct-to-patient marketing and did most of their acquisition through that model. We've also built the prediabetes centers, TEXAS Metabolic Centers, all focused upon management of pre-diabetic and diabetic conditions. More recently, we've supported continuous glucose monitoring and insulin pump companies as well by locating, then educating and counseling patients on the concept of CGM.

Durable Medical Equipment: In contrast to direct-response TV commercials, our navigation process refers to a local dealer for a "test drive."

Endocrinology: Our navigate process is different than traditional direct-to-consumer advertising. We observed this in endocrinology brands in conditions like osteoporosis. .

Genetic Risk in Men's Health: Clients have engaged us to reach men to consider diagnostic alternatives, as well as new treatment technologies for prostate cancer.

IV Hydration Market: We have created integrated programs for outpatient retail-type practices in which high levels of infused nutritional vitamins, minerals, and trace elements are infused through IV, to reverse fatigue and other sorts of chronic, non-life-threatening conditions.

Oncology: We've supported providers who focus on oncology, particularly in genetics and genetic risk for prostate cancer and breast cancer.

Ophthalmology: Our process has supported work for macular degeneration testing. This has been helpful for well patients who were virtually legally blind, for example, providing high-amplification glasses that gave them the ability to see.

Rare Diseases: This process becomes even more relevant for patients with rare diseases. such as hereditary angioedema, acromegaly, clotting disorders, or eosinophilic esophagitis.

Prototypical Patient: Susan's Support Pillar

After discussing all of the steps and treatment options with Anthony, they agreed to let Meg arrange an appointment for Susan with a local specialist. When Meg called, she assured Susan that all of the specialists with whom they were partnered had years of experience treating OAB patients. They would run diagnostic tests to determine the best and most efficient course of action to take to bring Susan relief as quickly as possible.

Next, she explained what you could expect to happen at the first appointment and offered to help Susan write a list of questions to ask the doctor. "Is there anything else I can help you understand better?" Meg asked. Just knowing someone truly wanted to help made Susan feel better. She didn't feel so alone any more.

"No, thank you, Meg. You have helped me and my husband so much already. We are very thankful."

Five days later Susan sat in a pretty blue and gray waiting room, prepared to meet Dr. Benjamin Allen. She was holding her notepad, the brochure, a pen, and a list of specific questions that Meg had helped her write.

She was a little nervous but felt confident she had come to the right place when Dr. Allen introduced himself and firmly shook her hand. He was personable, looked her in the eyes, and smiled warmly, reminding Susan of her youngest son, David. Best of all, Dr. Allen assured her they would have her feeling much better as quickly as possible. He had been trained in the latest OAB technologies and treatments. And she believed him.

Chapter 6:

Step 4 = Advocate

Having gone through Locate, Educate, and Navigate, why wouldn't you just stop at the appointment? That was the goal, right? We wanted to get the right patient to the right intervention at the right time with a focus on the right outcome. Why not just say, "We did our job, and that was good enough?"

That depends on what you define as your job. I define our job at 83bar and patient activation as bringing patient awareness and engagement to innovative medical products and services. To do that successfully, we need to make sure we complete the entire process.

Completing the entire process to me means helping people so much that they will not only want to be vocal and help others, but they will be equipped to do so! It's the concept of "pay it forward." A lot of times people go through experiences and say, "Wow, that was really good. I really enjoyed that," or "I really feel better." But they don't know what to do next. They're not self-empowered. They just don't know what the next tools are.

Advocate follows two concepts:

- It finds the patients who had a good experience and gives them the tools to be able to help others and pay it forward.

- It also finds the patients who haven't had a good experience and provides a means for taking corrective action so that they can have a better experience.

If you do that, you've completed a 360-degree loop in your customer service around the patient. You are more likely to get better amplification and better congruency in the marketplace.

Perhaps you, too, have read books and listened to podcasts which assert that in this age of consumerism, many people often either write reviews or post blogs about products or services. Everybody wants to share their experience as an empowered consumer. What are they saying about you?

The age of decentralized authority

We used to rely on guides, at some point, like Consumer's Digest. Think about that today; if you intend to buy a car, the last thing you want to do is read a magazine from a bunch of people who are literally getting paid by manufacturers to write reviews.

The reality today is that we are distrustful of authority figures in general. This follows the degradation of our government and everything else that we've been dealing with as a society. Trust is going down, while the empowerment of people is going up. Consequently, we tend to trust our friend "Jessica Jones" or even a guy named "Tommy T" on Yelp more than we trust a physician, society in general, or some governmental body.

Ultimately, the rise of Yelp means I don't have to trust food critics on restaurant choices; therefore Zagat is not what it used to be. However, I do trust my neighbor who has gone to a restaurant, along with all of the rest of her neighbors who have gone there and have written reviews about the place.

Basic customer follow-up is a new idea

In this last step of the Patient Activation system, Advocate, we have a post-consult follow-up. It may seem so basic, but in health care it is being treated like a new idea. If I have an oil change, the quick-lube dealer calls me the next day to ask, "Were you happy with our service? How would you rate us on a scale of one to ten? Is there anything we could do better?" If I take my dog to the vet, they call me the next day. But somehow it is new in health care consumerism to ask, "How did your appointment go?" and "How are you feeling this morning?"

I think this attitude has been driven by the fact that, if you think about the usual health care consumer experience over the course of the last thirty years, it has gone from having the local town doctor know your family to having a stranger barely know your name. When I grew up, I had a doctor named Dr. Waznick. He took care of my mother, my father, me, and my brothers. We ended up going to that doctor for the first fifteen to twenty years of our lives, He was sort of the central point, a respected authority in our lives.

But over the course of time that kind of relationship with a family doctor has dissipated if not disappeared altogether. That centralized authority figure certainly has vanished for most families and we've been left to try to understand health care issues on our own as we look for answers that are no longer curated for us.

And think about the doctor. They were once paid an appropriate amount of money and if you saw their schedule it was probably one patient every half an hour, so they'd see two patients an hour. Over the last twenty years that has been condensed. We now expect physicians to treat six patients an hour, so that consult time of thirty minutes has been reduced to eight-to-ten minutes. It has certainly changed the dynamic of the relationship. Somewhere along the way, we've lost the family doctor and we've created the factory. Like all factories, it is all about production.

Doctor sees you, figures out what you want, decides what prescription he must write, gets out the door, moves to the next room. that is why physician offices have one door lined up after another: it's all logistically planned so they can get through appointments more quickly. When you think about it, it reminds you of the early evolution of any type of automation. It's all focused on high yield production, never on satisfaction. That has become secondary.

Only now have we started seeing the evolution of concierge medicine. We see people no longer willing to be treated like cattle; there are alternatives now! Health care has begun to adjust and many have adopted the model of saying, "Look, we just can't process people. We actually have to reconsider what we're doing. And we have to adapt our practice afterwards."

Now we are moving towards a world in which the doctor and the hospital are going to be compensated and incentivized based on patient satisfaction. The ACOs and the CMS are going to come around and say, "If the patient wasn't happy, and if they didn't have a positive outcome, you'll be penalized. If they did have a good experience and they had a great outcome, you're going to be rewarded." How does that change the nature of how you think about patient satisfaction? Instead of a "nice to have," now it really is part of your remuneration.

The key thing is that if you don't have patients prepared, you are literally trying to fix the car at sixty miles an hour. The patient coming in unorganized, unprepared, doesn't know what the issues are, isn't straightened out, is going to cause chaos in your system. The likelihood of getting a negative result, or a negative satisfaction level, is significantly higher than when you treat the person who is coming in who's got a framework of understanding about what happens next, what they're expected to do, and what a good outcome is like.

The doctor as a mechanic

Have you heard the analogy that a doctor is like a mechanic— looking under the hood of the patient? Even the eye contact feels like that sometimes because they're so busy trying to click it all out on the EHR. They're looking at the iPad and the computer instead of looking at the patient, so even the dialogue with the patient is different in this new setting.

I have a personal opinion on that as somebody who's well-versed in technology and has been an early adopter my whole life. I think the adoption of EMR systems into health care has been treacherous. I began to see it in my previous health care business, when we started to adopt a digital framework. For patients with high complexity, there is something to be said about just sitting at a table with a pen in hand, listening, writing, listening, writing, listening, writing. There's something sort of cathartic about that. And it's revealing. And it's very personal. We noticed that when we saw the technical influence of clicking boxes and templatest, we started to lose the art of medicine. Diagnosing and treating patients became more the art of the process, the Medicaid protocol, or algorithm monitoring.

Technology is going to be here, so there's not much we can do about it. But we must not forget the effect of sitting across a table looking at a person, reading the body language, consuming the information in bite-size pieces and writing it down. The act of physically writing it down in front of them, where they can actually see what you're writing, has a more reassuring and soothing effect upon the patient. It is more interactive and human than when they watch you hold a terminal, the screen of which only you can see, and you just keep clicking boxes off because you are trying to quickly go through some templated form for an algorithm.

It's like a lot of other things in our lives. How many times have you gone to a restaurant where you have seen two people sitting at a table, both on their iPhones the entire time, not speaking to each other. If you were to ask those people, they might say they were "in the moment" with each other and they are basically just taking care of their multitasking. They feel like they're having dinner with somebody. What it doesn't look like from the outside is that they are even communicating.

Now take that one step further and say I'm going to give you an iPhone if you go out to dinner with your wife tonight, but she will not have a phone; at dinner you're on your iPhone while she sits there looking at you. I think that is somewhat the feeling people get in conversations with their physician now.

Patient Activation: "Pay it forward"

The patient comes in prepared and knows what she wants and can walk through the process quickly; she is ready to get the doctor's help in deciding what is important. Together, they narrow down that engagement to a couple key points. Then, the iPad is still not great, but better for the person who knows what she wants and knows she is a few steps away from getting where she needs to be versus the one who's wandering.

The idea is we want to give some positive empowerment to patients. Then, we can amplify that through social media.

That is a big part of the Advocate step.

There is no gaming the social media whatsoever. If the patient says, "Look, I had a good experience; I'd like to share my experience with others," we can send them a toolbar. With the toolbar will be a link to the Yelp page, a link to that practice's Google page, and so forth. All the links they need will be there so they can fill out the appropriate review and leave commentary for others to read and share. Having that all assembled in one email where they can just click through and do it immediately and properly is a significant step in compliance versus having people go out and search for these things one by one.

We don't want to put any words in anybody's mouth, and you certainly don't want to make it contrived. What we're looking for is honest, transparent referrals, or honest, transparent opinions expressed by patients who truly had a good experience and want to help others;

they want to pay it forward and we provide the means. If we do that, we've accomplished what we set out to do.

What if corrective action is needed?

Say someone had a neutral, or even worse, a negative experience. How do we circle back? How do we capture those experiences?

We're either on the phone with the patient after they've been through the consult, or we're actually doing some sort of feedback loop via either a text message or an email that is coming back to us with a response to a rating system. And if somebody rates a provider "moderate" or "low," we will reach out and ask, "What is the problem? What was the issue? How can we correct it?"

Think about what happens now. Somebody goes to a physician or somebody goes to get a medical procedure. It doesn't go well. They go home disgruntled and they will typically tell ten other people that they did not have a good experience. But they never really tell the provider because who goes back into a doctor to tell him? You can't get an appointment for three or four weeks anyhow; besides, what do they care? That is the perceived mentality: "What do they care?"

The reality of it is, if a provider knew, they probably would care, and if they had a mechanism that they could use to actually help somebody better, they would probably care even more. So the idea is to maintain contact with that person and then act as their advocate and say, "Okay, you haven't had a good experience; how do we make it right?" Then we work with the provider to make sure that it gets taken care of.

There are incentives for all parties to participate in this process. The patient wants to have a better experience and get it off their chest. The provider has worked hard and doesn't want bad reviews. If we intercede, they won't get bad reviews.

83bar is highly motivated to ensure success because 83bar is the entity who put these two parties together, and we want to continue to be the connecting party to help more people. We are only going to succeed at doing that if we continue to provide a rock-solid product and service with which both parties win.

You might wonder how the physician feels about the feedback going to 83bar and how we report it back to the doctor's office.

All physicians at some point think they could do all these important things themselves. After a few weeks of trying, they realize that they have zero ability to do this.

Here are some reasons why:

They typically are open three to four days a week. They have limited hours. They have front desk staff who are trying to get in and out as quickly as possible. Complaints take time. And by the way, most people who aren't happy are working and they really want to contact you at night, anyhow. Often times, when they do contact you, it'll be on voicemail. When the world explodes at nine o'clock in the morning when that doctor's office opens, the last thing that gets taken care of every day is voicemail; it may be days or weeks before complaints even get addressed, if they get addressed at all.

This is why they finally realize they don't have the skills or the bandwidth to take it.

So, we not only gather the feedback, we also report back with an aggregate, "Eight out of ten people were happy but these two people weren't and here's what they said. And here's what you can do about it."

Here's a classic example of a typical incident.

We have a client who does genetic breast cancer risk testing. Most of that testing occurs at an OB/GYN. What happens is, if you're an OB/GYN, the most important thing you do is deliver babies. Babies don't have a time clock on them, so they basically come whenever they want to come. They want to be delivered whenever they decide it's going to happen. What ends up happening is OB/GYNs cancel large portions of their schedule frequently. It's just the nature of the practice.

If you think of the doctor who cancels an entire Saturday because three babies were delivered and one had complications, that entire Saturday schedule has to be rescheduled. Somebody who is coming in for genetic testing is certainly low on the priority scale of ever getting rescheduled.

So what we know happens—and we've seen this over and over and over again for this particular client—the patient scheduled for the test is all set. They get canceled at the last minute. They were told they would get called back again but no one ever calls them back. A week goes by, two weeks go by, they forget about it. Someone else in their family gets breast cancer; someone else gets a lump; they get scared. All of a sudden, six to eight weeks have passed; now they're trying to figure out where they had an appointment. They've got to try to call again; it's another six weeks to get on the appointment list.

By the way, they may get canceled again and now they're on the cycle. Now it's six months or a year later and their sister has breast cancer. They literally are in a high target zone that you could have done something about.

What we do is different.

By doing that feedback loop consult, we reach out. We ask, "How did the appointment go?"

The patient tells us, "It didn't go. They canceled me at the last minute."

"Have they rescheduled you?"

"No."

"Okay, sit still, we're going to call you right back. We're going to get you right back on the schedule."

Because we have a working relationship with the offices, we get them right back on the schedule. We continue to follow up and there are no big gaps.

Prototypical Patient: Susan's Purpose - Perpetuation of Great Health Care

Later that afternoon Susan walked through the front door of her home, set down the groceries and her new prescription, and called Anthony, who had not yet returned home from work. She happily told him that she was feeling better already, just knowing there was hope that she would soon be well, and had just hung up after saying goodbye when the phone in her hand rang. Meg asked, "How did it go with Dr. Allen?"

Susan was pleased to describe how approachable and kind the doctor had been. "He didn't rush me! He answered all of the questions on my list and made me feel like he really cared about helping me get well." Meg could hear Susan's smile across the miles. "It was wonderful to feel like he was really listening to me."

"That is wonderful, Susan! I am so glad you were made to feel comfortable and that he answered all of your questions. Have you thought of anything else that you would like me to answer for you?" Susan said she had not.

Next Meg let Susan know that she would be sending her an email right away that would have a link to a page through which Susan could leave a review of her experience in Dr. Allen's office, if she wished. The happy mother and wife assured the friendly nurse that she would love to. "Thank you, Meg!" Then she hung up and immediately dialed her aunt, for she could hardly wait to tell her the good news that there was hope for her recovery, too!

Business implications

In marketing, the Net Promoter Score is derived from two basic questions:

- Would you buy this product again?

- Would you refer it to a friend, family, or colleague?

The Net Promoter Score (NPS) was created by Dr. Fred Reichheld and documented in his Harvard Business Review articles and in his book, *The Ultimate Question. Driving Good Profits and True Growth.*

Dr. Reichheld writes, "There's economic power in high-quality relationships." To understand the connection between creating advocates and growing your practice or brand, it starts with a simple fact. Just like in other kinds of businesses, every decision for patients ultimately involves an economic trade off. Every health care organization wants better relationships with its patients—but at what cost?

"Building high-quality relationships does cost something, often a considerable amount. It requires investment, it requires reducing an organization's reliance on bad profits. The real question is not just the cost but the benefits and how one stacks up against the other," suggests Dr. Reichheld. Health care companies need to understand the economic value that results from building better patient relationships. They must be able to answer questions such as these:

What would it be worth to raise our NPS by ten points? Where would this improvement show up in our financials? At the moment, few managers can answer these questions. Using the data that 83bar can generate, we help our clients understand.

To begin to understand, look at high-quality customer relationships and how they transform the economics of retailing. Costco, the wholesale club company, boasts an NPS of 79% and has grown to 45 million members despite spending little on advertising or marketing.

While a typical big box supermarket carries 40,000 SKUs, Costco stores have only 4500, carrying only those items with which it can provide outstanding value. Sales per store are almost twice those at Walmart's Sam's Club, its closest competitor. Costco's success funds a generous compensation package for its employees. New hires start at $10 an hour, which is high for the retail industry, and they can earn $40,000 a year after three years.

They receive a benefits package virtually unequaled in the industry. Low turnover and long tenure reduces hiring and training costs and boosts productivity. They also contribute to Costco's remarkably low inventory shrinkage rate, which is only 13% of the industry average. The company eliminates bad profits through a generous return policy: there is no time limit on returns (except for electronics and major appliances, which have a 90-day return policy with receipt).

Costco's earnings grew at 16.5% a year from 1994 to 2004 while its stock price gains exceeded 20% a year. The storyline is much the same at every company that has built communities of good relationships. Enterprise Rent-a-Car charges less than competitors, pays its employees far more, and has grown so fast that it is now the largest single buyer of cars and light trucks in the United States.

Chick-fil-A was able to grow nearly 15% annually between 1994 and 2004 despite ranking near the bottom of its industry in national marketing expenditures as a percent of sales. The company generates superior profits in the price-sensitive fast food business while helping the average operator of a free-standing restaurant earn more than $170,000 a year, far more than comparable managers and competitors.

Both companies have recorded NPSs well above the rest of the industry. Clearly, superior relationships drive economic advantage in ways that leave the competition mystified.

As Dr. Reichheld says, "Let's strip away the mystery. The value of an advocate can be quantified. Given the vital role of word-of-mouth, indeed it must be quantified. You may not have all the data you need at your fingertips but most companies are able to produce it. If exact figures aren't available, use reasonable estimates."

The first step is to calculate the lifetime value of your average patient. The fundamental approach is to tally up all the cash flow that occurs over the life of a typical patient relationship and then convert this total into today's dollar value. The next step is to understand that the lifetime value of an average patient, by itself, may not be all that useful. In fact, advocates exhibit dramatically different behaviors and produce dramatically different economic results.

The lifetime value is just the beginning of metrics. Several other factors can be considered when estimating the economic effect advocates have on your practice or brand:

- retention rate

- margins

- annual spend

- cost efficiencies

- word-of-mouth

The challenge of measurements

One challenge for many companies is that teams frequently reorganize. Furthermore, as presented in The Ultimate Question, a single hospital patient may interact with a case manager; professionals in nutrition, oncology, anesthesiology, physical therapy and radiology; multiple nursing shifts; and administrative services. Each department assigns staff to each patient, so how can you track the effectiveness of each small team that forms around each customer? You can't ask a patient to fill out a survey after each blood test or radiation treatment.

Cancer Treatment Centers of America, CTCA, a chain of specialized oncology hospitals, came up with a clever solution to this problem. It is reworking its patient care tracking system to register which departments and which employees from each department touch each patient. Scores are gathered from the patient and, when applicable, from their family caregiver at the end of each hospital stay.

The methodology will allow CTCA to compute an NPS for every department and every staff member, just as sports teams collect statistics to measure each player's contribution. In basketball, the point differential compares the team's points for and points against when a player is on the floor, with the same numbers when he or she is on the bench. Each department can benefit from this kind of feedback.

For example, it will be possible to determine which staff oncologists are generating the most enthusiastic patients and promoters. Since referrals are vital to the success of the institution, these exemplars merit careful observation so their practices can be documented for training other staff physicians. By focusing both front-line and board member attention on delighting patients, CTCA has achieved eye-popping results with its internal survey, reporting NPS results in the low 90% range.

Steve Bonner, a director and former CEO for CTCA, explained it this way. "The move towards operationalizing NPS is allowing us to remove the complexity associated with measuring and managing customer loyalty. The results look promising while extending our track record of four consecutive years of double digit revenue growth in a mature industry."

Measures of success must certainly go beyond functional or departmental effectiveness. They must be connected with the overall company values. In medicine, for instance, every institution strives for high-quality outcomes at the lowest possible cost but most institutions are measuring so many statistics for so many departments that they lose sight of the overall goal. What better gauge could there be than the percentage of patients who, as experienced consumers, would recommend a hospital, clinic, or rehabilitation facility to others?

Other ways of measuring growth

Some companies focus on market share and assume that if they are increasing their share they are satisfying more and more customers. But Dr. Reichheld suggested that market share alone means no such thing. Companies can increase their share for a while by buying growth through advertising, discounting, new marketing programs, mergers, acquisitions, and many other means but that doesn't mean they are in actuality delighting their customers. In fact, the contrary may be the case.

Market share leaders often use their power to milk customer relationships. When US Airways was new, the airline had to offer superior service and prices to attract customers, but by the time it dominated the Philadelphia market its executives thought it could get away with charging unreasonably high prices while letting service levels decline. Eventually, the company created so many detractors that it opened the door for Southwest Airlines to enter the market. Markets always balance.

PART III:

PATIENT ACTIVATION AT WORK

Chapter 7:

Applying
PATIENT ACTIVATION

Our exclusive 4-part activation system is integrated for:

- health care providers

- pharma companies

- medical device innovators

- ad agency partners

- media buying agencies

- consultancies

These are some of our partner specialists: Urologists, Urogynecologists, OB/GYNs, ENTs, Neurologists, Cardiologists, Gastroenterologists, Colorectal Surgeons, Dental Surgeons, and Functional/Integrative Medicine Physicians

What daily struggle in their practice do they all have in common?

A lack of time.

In the constantly shifting consumer medicine landscape, physicians are under more pressure than ever to do more with less. This means more patients per day and less time available to educate patients on advanced treatment options. Consequently, they are faced with the choice between practice evolution or extinction.

How does 83bar help?

By locating, educating, and navigating prepared patients directly into our partner provider specialist practices, we are increasing practice efficiency and throughput. This is mutually beneficial for the patient and the provider because patient prospects have already been pre-educated about advanced diagnostic, medical device, or treatment options prior to their time with the physician. This shortens the conversation, allowing the physician and patient to focus directly on the appropriate next steps in the pathway for that particular patient.

Remember the four parts of the Patient Activation system:

Step 1 = Locate

Step 2 = Educate

Step 3 = Navigate

Step 4 = Advocate

When one thinks about patient activation, imagine what could possibly change the paradigm of the current health care structure and actually solve most of its economic problems.

My experience in fibromyalgia and fatigue centers taught me that patients often saw many doctors and spent many, many thousands of dollars before they got to us. Sometimes it was only after they had already spent lots of time and money that they found us and we were able to help them.

The problem is that they were left to their own devices in a health care system that is so highly fragmented, they literally were bouncing from one place to another, trying to find help. There was no organized system to help them and no one to guide them. There was no transparency, as there rarely ever is in health care. When they did reach us, they felt a sense of relief that they had finally found somebody who actually understood their problem.

I can't imagine those experiences of seeking treatment for fibromyalgia and fatigue are any different from the experience of a patient seeking help with procedures for any type of non-mainstream sore throat or earache, and they occur daily. So, what you have is a significant level of inefficiency in the marketplace. Patients wander self-guided and self-directed in a fragmented system that many of the care providers inside the system don't even really understand, and about which no one can really give a complete answer. Moreover, when it comes to medical records, even though we've been promised systems could be integrated across treatment settings, we still do not have EHRs that talk to each other.

So, how do we solve inefficiency and how do we solve cost overruns? Well, we make it an efficient system. An efficient system would be getting the right patient to the right place for the right interaction at the right time. If we could do that quickly and efficiently, we would cut down the cost structure and create a much more frictionless environment.

We constantly surveyed our patient base in the fibromyalgia and fatigue centers. What we learned in that process is that the typical patient had been to eight doctors over the course of three and a half years before they got to us and they had spent north of $8,000 to $10,000 in copays and deductibles alone. that is a fair amount of money to spend and still be unsatisfied. It's a significant amount of time to spend and still be unsatisfied. When you compound the time, the frustration from the inefficiency as they spent time trying to manage this, and the actual hard money they'd spent, it's an incredibly inefficient system and an incredibly unmanaged cost structure.

1. Direct responsibility for the cost of care is driving patients to become consumers

- Rising deductibles

- Rising co-pays Rising premiums =

- Rise of Self-Managed Health Care Consumer

2. Consumers view digital solutions as the most effective way to meet their health care needs

3. Unfiltered Masses

- Unqualified to answer questions

- Focused on financial qualification

- Limited customer service functionality

4. Inefficient Processes

- Baseline data collection

- Every patient is "not prepared"

- Patients bring own research to appointment

- Patient service expectations are rising

5. Reactive Not Proactive

- Patients unsatisfied & lack follow-up

- Negative amplified & positive unguided

- Practice loses higher margin patients

6. Unaligned Expectations

- Message consistency/positioning issues

- Poor education at patient engagement

- Product/service complexity needs time

7. Friction Filled Process

- Manufacturer to patient unguided = too many break points

- Can't tell 'story' during self-education

- Captive systems v's patient demand

8. Compromised Experience

- Patients unsatisfied & lack follow-up

- Negative amplified & positive unguided

- Practice loses higher margin patients

Here we have a significant opportunity. Getting the patient early on, helping them through the system, and making sure that they understand all of the choices empowers them, prepares them, and truly serves them. Getting them prepared to make the right decision, guiding them to the right place the first time, and assuring they get the right interaction is really what will change the dynamic of the current health care model.

Chapter 8:

Obstacles to
PATIENT ACTIVATION

What are the obstacles to making a patient or helping a patient go from a state of awareness in the brain as to what they have an issue and they want to do something about it to actually doing something about it?

What keeps a health care consumer from taking charge?

What we have found over the course of time is that there is no trusted source of curated information on the web or at anyone's disposal in virtually any means.

If you think about a clinician, a clinician has sources of truth: clinical textbooks, clinical papers, research manuals, and institutions. These sources of truth equip the clinician to find answers, and they become comfortable with these solutions.

For a patient it's much more random. It's a magazine article here, it's a tidbit there; you see this all the time as new studies get released. Every day the six o'clock news flaunts studies that tease and taunt: one day carbohydrates are good for you, the next day carbohydrates are not good for you. The reason they are so inconsistent is because they're pulling only selected pieces of information off of each recent research study and they're not telling us the whole story. They're simply sensationalizing choice components of it.

The prospective patient in the medical model faces this dilemma constantly. There is no one to guide them. They may be an electrical engineer by training, they may be a stenographer by training, they may be wholly competent in their respective fields, but whatever their background is, the bulk of them are not going to have a medical background. So there's no barometer or sense or trained intuition about whether something is true or not. They do not have an orientation towards the actual medical truth and because of this they begin the process with what we call "The Wild, Wild West" approach, which consists of going to Google (what we call Doctor Google), putting in symptomatology, and beginning that wild goose chase of finding article after article, following them wherever they happen to wander.

Quite frankly, the problem is staggering. If they put "fatigue" into a Google search engine, for instance, they will be presented with "solutions" suggesting everything from "You didn't sleep well last night" to "You're dying from cancer" and everything in between. That is not truly helpful for somebody who's truly sick. The typical person who has an issue does not know how to put their symptoms in a hierarchy, does not understand the correlation between grouped symptomatologies, and certainly doesn't understand the correlation between symptomatology and lab tests that they may be able to get from one of the public lab companies. They're at a huge disadvantage.

The other option they have is to go to somebody they know who has some limited medical knowledge and at least get some directional points. This tends to happen in the social media platforms quite often. You'll see many prospective patients begin to talk about what's bothering them with their circle of friends on Facebook or other social media platforms, where they feel they're in a trusted, proven environment.

When that happens they usually will get some level of truth but also some level of untruth, and it will all be driven by the individual's personal experience and their familiarity with all of the information they're interacting with. They don't have a reliable source of truth, for the information to which they are exposed is actually constructed based upon others' personal experiences rather than correlated or personalized for them to meet their needs.

Finally, they have the ability to engage the medical system but every time they engage the medical system several things happen:

First, they are confronted by a multi-tiered cost structure for each engagement. The first tier is they have to take time off from work or time out from what they're doing. There's a time cost.

Second, there's an inconvenience cost because they physically have to go from point A to point B to engage the health care system and that is not always simple. A simple general practitioner appointment at noon could mean leaving your job at eleven and getting back at two in the afternoon, missing half a day of work. Trying to coordinate your schedule around that can be quite frustrating as well as costly.

Third, they have a deductible in their insurance that they're going to have to meet. Since they're not dying (they think) and they don't feel their symptoms are bad enough, they really don't want to spend $200 or $300 for a visit that may result in nothing more than getting more lab tests ordered for them and then having to spend more money.

The fourth barrier is co-pays. Typically, somebody is going to order some sort of drug for them and then they'll be pressured to begin a regimen that is going to mean more expenditure on a recurring monthly basis. It is plain to see that there are at least four layers of cost and inconvenience to every one of these health care decisions. This is why they don't get made lightly.

In fact, these obstacles often stop patient activation. Some people never find the solution they need because they believe, "I don't know what I'm doing, I don't know who to ask, and if I go to and engage the health care system I'm going to spend money four different ways and it's going to be highly inconvenient."

Now, imagine that same person sees an 83bar campaign. They can fill out a form that doesn't cost them anything and they can take a ten-minute call that doesn't make them leave their house or reschedule their life, they are far more likely to get the help they need. They can speak to someone who has twenty years of experience and will listen with empathy, someone who can provide them with some level of reliable guidance because this person is a medical practitioner; they may not be a doctor or the script writer but they have a significant level of health care experience. They have a license to protect as they give guidance. At least the patient who interacts with an 83bar campaign has a shot at not going through the whole costly process over and over.

I have somewhat of an advantage over others because I at least have an idea of what questions to ask when I get to the physician; I have some semblance of direction and reasonable hope for progress towards acquiring an answer for the issue that I'm struggling with right now. It's vitally important to me that we help other patients find the right interventions at the right times to get the right outcomes.

Healthcare consumers have been "Primed"

Another factor to consider in the patient experience is what we call "Priming" of the consumer. Because of Amazon Prime, the patient as a consumer now has a different level of expectations. They expect every site to provide immediate responsiveness, credibility, empowerment, tools, videos, and calculators—all those types of features.

In twenty years, Amazon has been able to assemble an entire cohort of early adopters, aggressive decision makers, and people who are effective vocal advocates. Guess what? They buy twice as much, they shop twice as fast, and they happen to be 100 million people. Indeed, they just hit the tipping point: now 51% of United States households have been Amazon Primed.

That means Amazon Prime is conditioning patients to expect health care providers to conduct business the way Amazon does. They take care of daily business on Amazon and then come to you, expecting the same level of service, the same level of response.

But in the health care world, they have PPOs, insurances, co-pays, and the like. These things are routinely far more inconvenient than the typical Amazon shopping experience.

For Prime membership, they pay $120 a year and now think everything has a two-day turnaround. In some places Amazon already offers same-day services, but no matter where you live, it will be next-day very soon.

Such expedient convenience sounds great as a consumer, but how is it affecting all the other industries? Because those kinds of service are raising the standards of your customer. In health care in the past four years, providers have made people wait 30% more time to get the initial first appointment. It's now a full 24 days to get an initial appointment. You see the disconnect? It's huge.

So, marketing people who are tasked with getting people to move forward are working in a system doing the exact opposite of what consumers are being trained to expect every single day.

The system hinders patient activation

It's pretty simple. We live in an incredibly fragmented health care delivery model and it's mainly because there are the payers, the patients, and the providers. All three have different agendas, different needs, and different (usually conflicting) wants. It's still an artisan business. At the heart of it, a physician still practices the art of medicine. That is traditionally the delivery point. By practicing the art rather than the science of medicine, what you really have is a lot of one-off and a system resistant to process development. It becomes necessary to train prospective patients as they engage with the medical system over time.

When you were growing up and you went to the doctor, your parents took you to the doctor where they tried to figure out what's wrong with you. They sent you for lab tests, they gave you medication, you went to the pharmacy, and you got the medication. If it didn't work, you went back and you got another prescription. It went on and on and on. There was a lot of cause and effect, trial and error. that is just the way it happened. You always went to the doctor that your parents went to and occasionally that doctor referred you to a so-called expert.

Here's the problem with that system today: the physician that you and your family visit is trying to be an expert in a litany of ailments, conditions, causes, and diseases at the same time. General practitioners are overrun. Most of them have been out of school for thirty or forty years; they have earned CEU credits, but most have been educated by pharmaceutical reps (at best) to keep themselves updated in delivering.

The general practitioner today is almost in an impossible model. The payer is trying to keep costs down and therefore paying less and less for each code; so what's happening at the provider level is the provider has to go faster and faster. There is less and less time to get educated. Just think about it yourself. If you were treating fifty to sixty patients a day, by the end of the week you will have seen 250 patients for that week. Would you remember anything specific about each one of the patients you had seen? In fifty of those cases, it is possible that you didn't really learn with certainty what was going on with them. How do you prioritize those patients so that you can spend an extra ten hours (possibly available in your waking hours) to do research, to try to become a better physician for those particular patients and genuinely understand what their issues are to help them better?

Also during that ten hours you have to build a referral network. You have to understand who knows what they're doing, who's good at what in your triage area and you have to continue to attend conferences and earn CEU credits to keep your liability down and your education levels up and your certificates. It just becomes a no-win circumstance. The model is broken at the provider level.

The model is broken at the information level, too, because we practice defensive medicine all over the place because of lawsuits; everything's fraught with liability. Therefore, at the end of every commercial and at the end of every DTC announcement, there's a litany of things that could go wrong with taking a drug or going underneath a procedure. Part of that is because even though that may be the 3% or 4% outlier effect, it leads to defensive medicine; lawyers make you do it and in turn the FDA adopts it as a standard.

We end up in a situation where it is very, very difficult to get the right information at the right time because what we are getting has been filtered through a compliance and a legal lens first. Secondly it is forced through an educational lens and thirdly, it is profit-motivated. There is certainly not an impartial, transmittable pathway for quality information to flow to patients.

Finally, on the other side, the innovators who are trying to get products to market are hindered by the same encumbrances. It's very difficult to talk to Mary Jane Smith on 123 Main Street in an organized fashion. Lately, for the last twenty years, mass media and direct-to-consumer have been used to stimulate patient awareness.

The problem with these routes of communication is I could watch a TV commercial and get somewhat of an idea of what a drug may do and how it may help me, but I don't really understand enough to be able to be certain. I'm not educated, so when I go into the physician's office who has only seven or eight minutes to treat me, I begin asking questions and describing symptoms that haven't been properly prioritized. My questions clog up the appointment. I don't get my answers and it's poke and hope. It's the same old poke and hope that we talk about constantly in the model.

The system is inherently fraught with fragmentation, which makes it extremely difficult to get a patient from a sense of awareness to a sense of activation leading to a positive outcome. Instead, the system that typically gets followed results more often in six, eight, or ten attempts to achieve an outcome that is bearable or at least sustainable for some improvement in the person's life. Unfortunately, the optimum outcome is rarely reached.

Do doctors prefer passive patients?

I approach this topic with deliberate caution because the answer to this question can be quite cumbersome. It's very easy to be critical of the health care system in the United States and the validity of its delivery vehicle right now. It is tempting to lump physicians with lawyers and other professionals into a category of people whom we feel generally let us down. I don't think that is the case at all. We must resist such negativity.

Do physicians prefer passive patients over activated patients?

Passive patients who do not ask any questions (or who ask few) do not take as much time as patients who ask a lot of irrelevant questions. If they feel pressured to move quickly to the next appointment, doctors will consider activated patients who ask many questions to be high maintenance.

If we don't change the dynamic of the delivery model that now exists, physicians will continue to be forced to treat too many patients on a given day and they will continue to struggle with patients who ask a lot of questions. As patient activation increases, patients who are assertive and who no longer accept the norm are going to become more and more common. That will lead to very large traffic jams created in every physician's office.

Fortunately, something can be done about that.

If we're going to solve this economic problem in the health care delivery model, everyone has to participate. Patients have to take the time to become better educated; it is their responsibility. They have to be self-prepared and they have to act like consumers. Currently, the average consumer spends less time figuring out who's going to perform their heart surgery than they do buying a pair of shoes or a coat. They certainly conduct less research, and that is just ridiculous.

So if the patient takes more responsibility for the process and the physician takes more responsibility for being directly educated and somewhat specialized in their delivery model, we can improve the process until physicians can change their outlook on patients who ask a lot of questions. Such patients no longer have to be considered high maintenance and detrimental to their treatment process.

Physicians go to school because they care about helping patients get better. They continue their education so that they can improve. They don't go to school to process and put bolts on a machine like a factory worker. that is not what they spend their life educating themselves for. They genuinely want to help people. But we have to create a better environment where they can actually help people and that is going to take adjustments. It takes two to tango. Patients must be better prepared, able to select and prioritize their questions, and physicians must maintain an environment in which they can focus and respond.

I remember reading a *New England Journal of Medicine* article about five or six years ago. It described how the traditional general practitioner walks into a room and spends about a total of eight minutes, but of that eight minutes, two minutes is spent picking up the chart, chit-chatting with the nurse on the outside, and scanning the chart before they walk in so they can get their game face on for having a conversation. They are already formulating in their mind what they're going to do, then they talk to the patient. The patient doesn't know how to organize their symptomology at all. I remember reading in the article that the number one condition people talk about is being tired all the time. They complain, "I'm fatigued," but that really doesn't help anybody diagnose anything.

The third, fourth, or fifth symptom mentioned is often the most important symptom in your diagnosis. However, it has also been found that physicians typically begin to make up their mind and stop listening by the time the patient has mentioned the third symptom. They are beginning to write a prescription before the fourth and fifth symptom are even out of the patient's mouth. Before you know it, they are preparing to exit.

In their head they have already begun to have the conversation, "Okay, I've got two minutes left. I've got to get out the door. I've got to make sure I get the notes written, get this patient taken care of and move on to the next one." They continually think ahead like this because they know as soon as they get delayed by ten or fifteen minutes, the whole waiting room will start to back up and everyone's experience will deteriorate.

So you have a clash of mechanics there. The patient doesn't know what to ask. They're not prepared. They don't know how to prioritize their symptomatology and the physician is trying to proceed in a structured way so that they can make very important but rushed reasonable decisions before they have to move on as quickly as possible to stay economically viable. that is not a delivery model that will provide solid great medicine. So it has to change, and it has to change on both sides.

Objections to the 83bar sales system

Some manufacturers, diagnosticians, medical device manufacturers, and therapeutic companies do not agree that the system proposed by 83bar can solve the problems crippling the current health care system. Their objections generally fall into one or more of three specific categories:

1. We haven't done that before.

2. We do not want to alienate our physicians.

3. We have our own internal staff.

"We haven't done that before" is the protest of companies who resist change, even if change ensures progress. The idea is that the marketing team has always been in charge of awareness and the sales team has always been in charge of conversion and activation. Never do the two cross, regardless of the cultural corporate speak that everybody uses when they talk about how they are all one team who works together. They really don't work together. So you have the marketing department saying, "We raised awareness. We did our job" and you have the sales department saying, "We don't have enough people aware of the product, so it makes it harder to sell." There is the conundrum.

When 83bar presents its system, it must be embraced as a completely integrated process, from the idea in someone's head all the way to the final sales solution and post-feedback loop. This happens when someone earnestly says we're going to do it all and we're going to have it underneath one software platform. We're going to be able to track it and we're going to be able to hold people accountable for the delivery module. that is certainly touching on new ground inside of a corporate culture.

In progressive, aggressive corporate cultures, it is something they embrace. In more traditional, more staid, and more protective corporate cultures, it is something they tend to rebuff early in the discussions.

"We do not want to alienate our physicians." This one is the most confounding, because it's a real disconnect between marketing and sales again. The sales people have the relationships with the physicians and they have very tight relationships usually, so everything revolves around not disrupting the power balance between the salesperson and the physician who's ordering. Marketing is relegated to the backseat, where they are told, "Look, just do your duty. Don't get in the way of the real sales activity that happens out here."

A problem occurs if you remove the emotional bonds and friendships that tie sales reps to ordering physicians because... again, remember, these are all transient relationships... the reality is that in the case of most diagnostics, therapeutics, and devices, the ordering physician is actually the order fulfillment for the company, and they do it for free. You're marketing and you're selling the product, and ultimately at the end of the day, that physician orders that product, places that product, and refers that product to patients, but they don't really get anything out of it, except for the betterment of the patient. There's nothing wrong with that; it can be quite altruistic, but in reality what we ought to be doing is we ought to be thinking about how to make that physician's job easier, simpler, more effective, and more conducive to their workflow.

The most significant thing a company can do for its physicians is to educate and prepare each patient so when they walk into the physician's office or a point of delivery, they are prepared, knowledgeable, and ready to act. If you do that for a physician, then you've made their ability to deliver a positive outcome significantly better. You've made the physician-patient interaction significantly better, and you've certainly made their day a lot better.

A company trying to build a long-term vision of how to go to market will understand that they are in a competitive slice. A successful one will commit to their physician partners over the long haul; they will say, "Look, we're going to do the heavy lifting and make sure the patient understands the benefit of what we're selling. We're going to make sure the patient understands the value of you, the physician, in the delivery model. Finally, we are going to make sure that the patient post-visit or post-treatment is not going to be calling your office twenty times afterwards and creating additional work for you."

If you do that, to a physician you're a great partner. You're a great partner because you're bringing them ready-to-act patients who are educated. Oftentimes they'll monetize those patients in multiple different ways and have a great relationship with them. The relationship will not start with, "Hey, I saw this on TV and I want this." When that happens, the relationship often starts with disappointment or disagreement. "Well, it's not really appropriate for you," then the patient's begins to get upset and may even threaten to go to another doctor. This kind of interaction happens when patients believe the doctor is merely a distribution point instead of a partner.

"We have our own internal staff" is the objection often given by providers who don't see value in the fully integrated 83bar system. They have someone who answers the phone and provides customer service, or they use a call center. It is mystifying to us how this can be a logical objection considering the fact that most call centers are staffed as an early entry job. They typically do not hire senior-level people. They're certainly not clinically versed people.

Moreover, they're often providing minimal assistance on the phone for these companies that have large expenditure items. Finally, they're usually only available during normal business hours. So it is an inferior system.

- inferior talk track

- provided only during normal business hours

- provided by a nonclinical person who has very little empathy and is doing an entry level job

How is that more efficient and cost-effective than having twenty-year, battle-tested, experienced nurses serve your patients?

A physician locator is a perfect example of how not to be first and fast, for they often fail at being responsive to your clients or prospective patients. Most medical devices and therapeutics companies list participating physicians who provide services on their behalf, as in a partnership. They also list the doctor's phone number.

The trouble is most doctors are barely working forty hours a week. When they do, oftentimes the desk is too busy to answer the phone, so all this money has been spent on building a physician finder only to find out than less than 2% of those phone calls ever get answered originally. Moreover, a very low percentage of people who leave a message ever even get followed up with. Too many times those calls go into the black hole at the front desk; they never get returned!

A prospective patient is deep in the funnel—ready to act and fully committed—wanting to book an actual appointment, but their attempt to reach the doctor proves to be completely ineffective. This happens because it is no one's core job to make sure the contact is completed. There's no one sitting there.

There's no partnership sitting there that ensures everyone gets paid. At 83bar, we stay viable in business by making sure there's a return on investment on these type functions. That is where we believe 83bar fills the gaps in and between all of the points of contact: We are fast, efficient, professional, empathetic, and responsive. Working with us, so are you.

Chapter 9:

The Impact of
PATIENT ACTIVATION

Measurable impact

More than 850,000 patient interactions indicate significant, measurable impact on the health care market.

Some people call it getting leads. We call it patient engagement, which is far more effective because it is when someone gets in touch with us, whether by going through one of our risk assessments or answering one of our health surveys, they provide a significant amount of information about the issues they're struggling with. We provide answers they are seeking! Then they provide us with their name, phone number, and email, and then ask us to contact them. The 850,000 we have helped are not just numbers on a list that has been randomly assembled. These are 850,000 people who have raised their hands, said, "I have a problem, here's my information, here's my name, here's my phone number, and please call me."

These are people who are truly committed to the process.

The key point is, whether we're involved in the process of educating patients about overactive bladder or we're in the process of genetic education navigation, patients are people and people want to feel like they have a level of control. If they feel like they have a level of control and they feel like they're being treated fairly, they will have a better experience. Furthermore, if they feel more confident that they know what they're doing because we have removed fear and risk from the decision process, they will typically feel they have had a better experience.

The takeaway is this: Just be brutally honest and blunt. Give people the tools they need to make the decision that is best for them. If you give them all the tools they need to make a decision, it will reduce their fear level. What you will see is faster decisions and better outcomes just because they're willing participants rather than people who are making decisions based on a wing and a prayer, hoping they did the right thing because they know they are really only guessing.

Let's think about lessons learned. What kind of bird's-eye view do we get from 850,000-plus patient clicks, leads, and discussions?

You get a sense of how broken the health care system is. The number one thing is people are generally trying to get an answer. They don't have primary care doctors anymore; they use the local urgent care center; they move around a lot. There's a whole bunch of reasons why the old system no longer exists. Even if they do have a primary care doctor, they can't get in often enough to actually have a conversation with them. Without any guidance, they are self-directed. When you are self-directed, as anyone knows, the minute you search online for symptoms or something that is bothering you, you're likely to feel like you're going to die within the next twenty minutes.

People enter the system in various ways. We try to get the right patient to the right provider at the right time to get the right outcome. That is not a linear process in health care right now. that is a process of hope and hope and hope some more. It literally is: hope you get to the right place, hope they can refer you to the right place, hope you get the right test taken, hope the right person is taking care of you, hope that person has experience in solving your problem. It's a completely unguided, uneducated, and un-navigated experience. that is health care today: highly fragmented and every person for themselves.

In summary, our value to marketers is far beyond simply adding "leads." Consider all the ways we can provide:

- incremental insights

- incremental leads

- incremental roi

- incremental patients

- incremental engagement

- incremental growth

Impact on providers and practitionersI ask myself, "How can I help these doctors?"

Consider why we are in this medical quandary.

When a physician graduates college, he enters "on-the-job" training. A fifty-year-old patient seeing a doctor in their peer age group, is being treated by a doctor who has not been in school for thirty years, except for CEU credits. The doctor's learning has been controlled and has aged thirty years. Moreover, they have no time to learn and their practices are now so focused on throughput, they don't really even have a life.

We used to have twelve toothpaste brands to choose from; we went to the store, compared brands in a minute, and bought the one we wanted then and there. Now we search Amazon and see 4,000 tubes of toothpaste and hundreds of different brands. We don't even leave our house. In that same time period, medical care has been delivered the same way. Consumerism has changed everything dramatically.

Why has this happened?

First, health care was paid for by funny money. If people had been paying cash for it all along, it would have changed in ways parallel to everything else.

It will take time to change the healthcare system. Meanwhile, though it seems our choices are endless, no one truly has any choice anymore because the only insurance anyone can really understand or pay for is one with a high deductible.

At some point (I'm shocked it hasn't happened already), mass numbers of patients are going to say to themselves, "Okay, I go to the doctor once a year for ten years and maybe I am on one blood pressure medication. Look at how much I am spending. My insurance has cost me over the course of ten years about $50,000 to $60,000 in premiums and then I have also paid, with deductibles and copays, another $10,000 to $15,000." They have spent $75,000 for the ten-year period while insurance has paid less than $10,000.

People live in fear of the heart attack that is going to cost them $30,000 or $40,000. They live in fear of what cancer could cost them. Perhaps $200,000, they think. The reality is, cancer costs $40,000 or $50,000. It's just a bill submitted for $200,000 that gets negotiated down to $40,000. If everybody knew that cancer really only costs $30,000 or $40,000, and a heart attack costs $15,000 or $20,000, we would be fighting a lot more over paying the premiums that we're paying right now.

When you were only paying a $150 or $300 deductible, the concern was probably suppressed. The problem now is you're paying a $5,000 deductible and $500-$600 per month for insurance. Even more discouraging is the statistic reported by a leading foundation that said there are about 60% of people who never hit their deductible every year — yet they pay $7,000-$14,000 in premiums on their policies. Employers are willing to pick up less of it, so now you're picking up thousands a year in premiums and paying the first $3,000, $4,000, or $5,000 of your deductible every year. This means you're never getting out of your deductible, and at the end of the year you are asking, "What did I just buy for $10,000?"

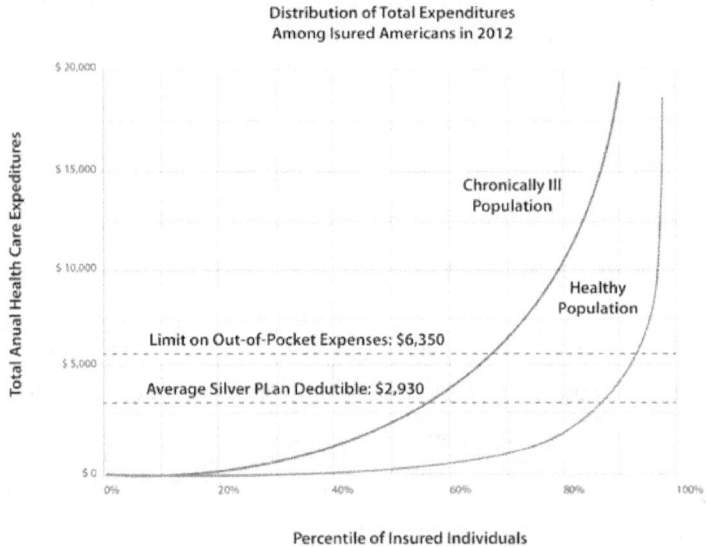

Distribution of Total Expenditures
Among Isured Americans in 2012

Now, consumers are beginning to ask questions. When the consumer asks the doctor these questions, they both naturally get annoyed. That is why Amazon Prime service sells so much. I don't have to leave my house, I don't have to get annoyed, and it shows up when I want it. Even better, I didn't have to pay for shipping. The expectation for similar "pain-free" transactions transfers to other parts of life.

If you're running a medical practice and you want to remain in business, you have two choices. You have the choice of adapting or becoming extinct. There is really no other choice.

An office that has not adapted will have two medical providers and four or five billing people. Everyone is miserable. An office that has adapted may have three medical providers and one clerical person to administer bookkeeping. They provide a much better product and the physicians can work probably seventy percent of the time they once worked and be happy.

You must figure out how to dynamically change your business so that it is consumer-oriented. Learn exactly how to deliver a product that people are willing to pay for, because they're not paying for it with insurance dollars anymore.

In fact, people in all walks of life want to make informed decisions without being afraid of making a mistake. If you want to continue to run the same way you did—on 27 different insurances—and you still want to do all the paperwork, then continue, but you're not going to be doing that much longer.

Impact on the health care consumer

You could do all the surveys you want and people are going to sometimes tell you the truth and sometimes tell you what they think you want to hear. Sometimes they're just annoyed with you, but at the end of the day there's no purer form of feedback than how people decide to part with their hard-earned money.

Over the course of the last fifteen years, the businesses we've operated and the businesses we've helped have conducted transactions totaling more than one billion dollars. These transactions range from a $50-per-month subscription to an IV company all the way to $53,000 for a full-mouth dental implant through a national dental implant provider.

According to the 10,000-hour theory, you develop expertise if you do something for 10,000 hours. We have 30,000-40,000 hours of experience and have certainly learned a lot about people while participating in transactions worth a billion dollars.

Everybody votes with their feet and with their wallet. Over time, transactions reveal trends; voting patterns indicate what clients truly want. Based upon those revelations, we built a product that is better for everybody. Subsequent voting patterns lead to improvement, resulting in continuous evolution.

The confusing world before 83Bar	The new world accelerated by 83Bar
• "What are my options?" • "Who is the best at treating this condition?" • "What symptoms are most important to highlight?" • "What should I track before my appointment?" • "Who takes my insurance?" • "How should I organize my thoughts for discussing this with doctor" • "Whom can I trust?" • "What questions should I ask my doctor?" • "What happens next?"	• Understands options and wants to discuss what is best • Ready for discussion of a hierarchy of symptoms • Understands what comes next • Understands payment framework • Has a game plan for discussion with doctor • Has background material ready for discussion with doctor

HOW 83BAR patient activation CAN MAKE A DIFFERENCE

- We filter, qualify, educate, and prepare prospective patients to act.

- We act as a bridge for innovators to help close user's information gap.

- Front desk strain is reduced, conversion goes up, and patients are better organized for their appointments.

- Friction is reduced between product and/or service knowledge and any associated transaction/s.

- This results in a better experience which 83bar helps amplify on behalf of the provider.

- Positive outcomes are amplified; negative ones are corrected.

Impact on the health care system

How could patient activation—and higher patient satisfaction—contribute to health care delivery in the US? Further implementation of accountable care organizations (ACOs) could provide an opportune leverage point.

As part of the Affordable Care Act of 2012, the Centers for Medicare and Medicaid Services launched ninety ACOs to provide and coordinate the health care of 2.4 million people in seven states. Private insurance companies followed suit. An ACO is an organization of health care providers, hospitals, clinics, and physicians that are reimbursed for providing and coordinating all of the health care used by a designated set of people who receive the plurality of their primary care from the ACO providers.

ACOs are responsible for the health care expenditures incurred by these people and, for an extra fee, the coordination of their care. Large insurance companies and self-insured employers have begun to experiment with making contracts with ACOs for the care of their insured groups, hoping that such coordination may reduce health care expenses without sacrificing quality.

By 2018, there were 561 ACOs, the majority of which were operated by large hospital systems or medical group practices.

The ACO model was originally envisioned to pursue what is called the triple aim:

1. Reducing health care cost

2. Enhancing patient experience

3. Improving population health

Translating this goal into a regulatory sphere, The Centers for Medicare and Medicaid Services named thirty-three performance indicators for which ACOs are financially rewarded.

As it relates to patient activation, it is interesting to note how many of the ACO model performance measures relate to patient satisfaction. These include:

- Getting timely care, appointments and information

- How well the doctors communicate

- The patient's rating of a doctor

- Access to specialists

- Health care prevention and education

- Shared decision making

- Receiving a wide range of coordinated care, preventive health screenings, and interventions for at-risk conditions

In their book, *The American Health Care Paradox: Why Spending More is Giving Us Less*, academic researchers Dr. Elizabeth Bradley and Dr. Lauren Taylor say: "While many see this as government intervention and investment in health care, it has also served to kick start private sector innovation in a variety of ways, including innovations from small business research and technology development."

Conclusion

On one level, the ideas behind this book are so simple, they're almost self-evident. Put most simply, the best way to ask for and receive better health care is to become a more activated patient. And the best way to deliver quality care is to create a more responsive, data-driven patient experience.

Although the pillars of our 4-part system may be surprisingly simple to comprehend, they can be difficult at first to execute day-in and day-out. It's what makes my job so challenging, yet so satisfying when we can help connect so many motivated and educated patients with so many caring providers.

Appendix

PATIENT ACTIVATION: Proposed Eco-System Scenario

Implementing a business model based on the Patient Activation System is uncomplicated.

Envision creating a fully integrated "ecosystem" in a pre-diabetes program. We would deploy our 4-part 83bar system for patients and HCPs.

1. Locate

Targeting consumers on social media based on our well-documented demographic and psychographic profiles, we identify prospective patients through brief risk assessment and health surveys. Our highly experienced registered nurses respond to them very quickly (usually within minutes).

We also target providers who specialize in pre-diabetes and those clinics who can offer comprehensive management. We invite them to join a program that makes patient marketing and administration more efficient and more effective.

2. Educate

Our nurses help educate, qualify, and screen candidates. Our nurse operators share relevant information to patients, offer meaningful solutions, and help them make informed decisions.

This is unlike traditional DTC media campaigns alone, because the nurse consultation raises patients from simple awareness to "ask your doctor" call-to-action. The educated patient is more prepared and motivated to act, then qualified for referral to a provider.

3. Navigate

Referring to the provider clinic network we've created, our nurses will guide patients to action through appointment scheduling or service fulfillment, whichever is appropriate. (We might even envision a way to have the new agent prescribed by our NPs, without an office visit.)

4. Advocate

We will offer comprehensive follow-up to ensure patient satisfaction with their experience, and to promote improved lifestyle and continued compliance. (Our ecosystem could offer a subscription model proven to work in chronic conditions that includes ongoing personal consultation, diet and exercise plans, and medication refills. This is designed to avoid the high drop- off rates seen with previous OTC products.)

This system is a concept that I have successfully employed in multiple businesses, including sale of products and procedures with price points from as little as $200 to about $7,000. It works—if you're willing to put in the work and commit to the process.

Building a predictable scale pattern

First, we will spend money going to the consumer masses to offer a free initial thirty-minute treatment evaluation to qualified individuals.

The intake form focuses on the key issues. "What is the reason you are seeking treatment in the beginning?" What we want to know is why they're actually showing up, what is bothering them, what in particular is bothering them, what they are missing out on because it's bothering them. Are they willing to make a commitment to a process to get better, because healing does not happen overnight? Their answer is key because some people will say, "No." These we'll flush out right away.

We also ask, what would they do in the future if we were able to help resolve their current health care issue? Finally, they are asked a personality-indexing question that we use with multiple clients; it allows us to speak using a tone that they understand. They will respond to the way we are talking to them.

We spend time carefully wording these questions so that we will get a high form-fill rate. In this case, we were looking for specific elements to determine whether a patient qualifies. If somebody doesn't have a key issue that is worthwhile for us to work on, then we probably would exclude them.. If somebody's not willing to make a commitment, we would cease consultation. We would inform them, "You just don't qualify."

The call to action is, "Do you qualify for a free initial thirty-minute treatment evaluation? We're so sure that what we do is good for you and life-changing—will help you with your health—that we're willing to make an investment in you. Are you willing to make an investment in yourself?" Statements like these are very effective, for they use principles of psychology and persuasion.

Within the first couple of weeks, our operators will contact everyone who has completed a form and qualifies, talking them through the process, working on any upgrades.

Five key issues are identified:

- What is the key issue driving this person to seek help?

- What is the hindrance that is stopping them now?

- What are they missing out on because of this key issue?

- If they feel better, what will be the change in their life?

- Are they willing to make a commitment to get that change in their life?

We will share this data with the therapist, along with the booking. In a perfect world, each day would start with the provider considering each one of these patients as an opportunity to change a life. He or she will decide that the conversation they will have with each patient is going to focus on mutual commitment. It should not be, "Come in and we'll give you a treatment and you'll like the experience; then when you go to leave, you should buy a membership." In that system, everything is driven by price and profit. I guarantee you, that is the race to the bottom. That is absolutely the worst position you could ever have.

Instead, the 83bar system is about demonstrating genuine compassion. "Hey, you filled this form out, you qualified for this, we made room for you. We're here ready to solve the problem that brought you here, because we know you're missing this. We know it's stopping this in your life, and if we get you better this is what we know will happen for you. We know you're willing to make the commitment." If we can have that conversation both internally in the room and then when they come out with the closer, you will be using their own words to persuade them. This strategy is incredibly powerful. It works.

We also ask questions designed to determine the prospective patient's personality-type. Four types of constituents are revealed with personality profiling. We covered these in the "Educate" chapter. There are four distinct personality types:

- The results-oriented person who prefers to have details short-versed, very direct, very blunt without a lot of flowery language. That person has a specific need. They prefer condensed information given to them very quickly.

- The analytical person who wants to know facts, numbers, and statistics. They make decisions based on data.

- The highly cooperative person is someone who avoids confrontation and does not like conflict, so they will be passive on the phone. You have to keep checking in with this type of person to make sure that they're okay and that they get all the information they need.

- Individuals who are a social personality type are very interested in testimonials, for they want to know who else has had it, used it, or done it.

As we take a look at the second part of the overall structure of this system, we remind you that patients self-select in. Based on the information they give us, we begin to frame the experience for them. For example, we send them information in between appointments, and the emails we send them have an appropriate tone and content to match the way they want to be talked to, based upon their personality type. This personalized communication frames what their expectations should be.

We make sure the data is gathered and passed in an organized, structured format. This data is only valuable if your staff uses it and it's only valuable if it becomes a standardized practice within your process. If it is not standardized, it will not work. Within the first 90-120 days of using the system, your process will become systematic, bugs will have been eliminated, and you will begin to see positive results.

Finally, you will have unified messaging. The therapist should have all of the information before they go into the room, so they can speak to the person the correct way. The closer should have all the same information. Everybody should be working from the same data plan. This should not be emotional, it should not be touchy-feely, and it should not be, "Well, this person likes me so I must be a great salesperson."

Ultimately you're crafting a solution based on all of those inputs; it's a customized solution, and from the prospect's point of view, it's like you have built it exactly the way they wanted it. What they forget is that they actually gave you the exact words you are using when you speak to them, but that is ultimately what works in a sales model.

Support mechanisms are at work in creating this success:

- we're doing the lead generation

- we have the contact center

- we perform the online scheduling

- we're sending communications that match

- we're building a customized persuasion pathway

So you see, we're getting five points of data, using it over five fragments, and building a customized solution for the patient.

Texas Metabolic Center provides four-month or year-long pre-diabetes programs. If you are pre-diabetic with A1C levels starting to climb up towards 6.5, you could join an all-inclusive subscription program with a symptom-oriented approach.

As a subscription member, a doctor would take care of you, you could get a prescription written, and you would not see the doctor again for six months, at which point you would probably need a modulated or changed prescription.

Texas Metabolic Centers wanted to condense the lengths of their programs significantly. They wanted to convey this message to their patients: "We are going to be with you every step of the way, not only getting you on the right medication, but also changing your diet and your exercise plan so that you can actually get a much better outcome. We're going to do that so you can go back to your life. You can go back to having control of your life as quickly as possible."

That subscription model works well with chronic diseases. It works well for both the provider and it works well for the patient. It is a typical model we have done patient acquisition for. For Texas Metabolic Centers, we identified patients who self-reported as having high A1C; we educated those who were struggling to manage it; and we navigated them to a comprehensive program that would manage it more efficiently and more effectively.

Recommended Reading

Blackett, Tom and Rebecca Robins eds. *Brand Medicine: The Role of Branding in the Pharmaceutical Industry.* New York: Palgrave, 2001.

Bradley, Elizabeth and Lauren Taylor. *The American Health Care Paradox. Why Spending More is Giving Us Less.* New York: PublicAffairs, 2015.

Christensen, Clayton M. and Michael E. Raynor. *The Innovator's Solution: Creating and Sustaining Successful Growth.* Boston: Harvard Business School, 2003.

Clifton, Rita, John Simmons, and Sameena Ahmad eds. *Brands and Branding.* Princeton, NJ: Bloomberg Press, 2004.

Fowles, J.B., P. Terry, M. Xi, J. Hibbard, C.T. Bloom, and L. Harvey. *Measuring self-management of patients' and employees' health: further validation of the Patient Activation Measure (PAM) based on its relation to employee characteristics.* Patient Education and Counseling, 2009; 77: 116-122.

Greene, J. and J.H. Hibbard. *Why Does Patient Activation Matter? An Examination of the Relationships Between Patient Activation and Health-Related Outcomes.* J Gen Intern Med. 2012 May; 27(5): 520-526.

Grosberg, D., H. Grinvald, H. Reuveni, and R. Magnezi. Frequent Surfing on Social Health Networks is Associated With Increased Knowledge and Patient Health Activation. J Med Internet Res. 2016 Aug; 18(8): e212.

Hendriks, M. and J. Rademakers. *Relationships between patient activation, disease-specific knowledge and health outcomes among people with diabetes; a survey study.* BMC Health Serv Res. 2014; 14: 393.

Loehr, Jim and Tony Schwartz. *The Power of Full Engagement: Managing Energy, Not Time, is the Key to High Performance and Personal Renewal.* New York: The Free Press, 2003.

MacLennan, Janice. *Brand Planning for the Pharmaceutical Industry.* Aldershot, England: Gower, 2004.

Martin, Patricia. *Rengen: The Rise of the Cultural Consumer - and What It Means to Your Business.* Avon, Massachusetts: Platinum Press, 2007.

Michelli, Joseph A. *The Starbucks Experience: 5 Principles for Turning Ordinary into Extraordinary.* New York: McGraw-Hill, 2007.

Reichheld, Fred. The Ultimate Question. Driving Good Profits and True Growth. Brighton, MA: Harvard Business School Press, 2006.

Simon, Françoise and Philip Kotler. *Building Global Biobrands: Taking Biotechnology to Market.* New York: The Free Press, 2003.

Smith, Shaun and Andy Milligan. *Uncommon Practice: People Who Deliver a Great Brand Experience.* Harlow, UK: Pearson Education Limited, 2002.

About Bob Baurys

Bob Baurys is a CEO, founder, advisor, investor, and fundraiser with a particular focus on health care, technology, and service sectors. Bob currently operates 83bar, LLC, and provides directional strategic guidance to The Gents Place, Texas Metabolic Centers, Replenish Hydration, Optimal Thyroid Program, and Trujay, LLC.

His bias is toward rapid growth and development while creating new market niches in technology-enabled health care and wellness fields. His core focus is on integrated client acquisition systems that combine speed, efficiency, and highly leveraged selling opportunities for health care-based partners.

Longtime clients and business partners say Bob has these core strengths:

- Thought Leader: developer of cutting-edge health care consumer concepts

- Start Up Specialist: from concept on a napkin to $10-$20 million in revenue

- Client Acquisition Pathway Builder: with a deep understanding of consumer behavior in health care space

- Reality Maker: experienced capital formation strategy, acquisition, and corporate structure/equity

- Leadership: developer of strong, critical thinking, risk-taking, and rapid-business-development teams

- Revenue Focus: firm believer that in startups, revenue is first and everything else is overhead

- Health Care Consumer Experience: deep understanding of cash medical services market (consumer-focused sales of $1 billion+)

- Strategy Development: marketing, sales strategy planning, deployment implementation

Bob currently resides in Austin, TX, with his wife, Claudette, and their three rescue dogs.

About Mark Stinson

Mark is a medical industry veteran in brand innovations, an experienced marketer, a translator of research, and a skilled group facilitator.

His work has included market assessment, branding, and marketing strategy for health, science, and technology products in pharmaceuticals, diagnostics, medical devices, provider networks, and clinical research tools.

Mark's career in marketing, communications, and branding spans some thirty years. He is founder and principal of Bioscience Bridge, LLC. Previously, he served as senior vice president of brand strategy at GSW. His career includes positions as president of a global brand consultancy, president and chief creative officer of an independent healthcare communications firm, and managing partner of an Omnicom medical ad agency.

Mark is a frequent speaker, trainer, and facilitator for sales meetings, advisory boards, and strategy workshops. He is the author of two business books, ForwardFast and N-of-8, and contributed to two motivational books, Living in the Now and Alone In My Universe.

Mark is a recipient of the Brand Leadership Award from the Asia Brand Congress for global marketing efforts. He was included in the PharmaVoice 100 Most Inspiring People in the Life-Sciences Industry.

Mark and his wife, Jenny, have five children and a golden retriever. They reside in Boise, Idaho.

www.ingramcontent.com/pod-product-compliance
Lightning Source LLC
Chambersburg PA
CBHW071455220526
45472CB00003B/809